GROWING

·IN·

PRAYER

DEVOTIONAL

MIKE BICKLE

**CHARISMA
HOUSE**

Most Charisma House Book Group products are available at special quantity discounts for bulk purchase for sales promotions, premiums, fundraising, and educational needs. For details, write Charisma House Book Group, 600 Rinehart Road, Lake Mary, Florida 32746, or telephone (407) 333-0600.

GROWING IN PRAYER DEVOTIONAL by Mike Bickle
Published by Charisma House
Charisma Media/Charisma House Book Group
600 Rinehart Road
Lake Mary, Florida 32746
www.charismahouse.com

Visit the author's website at www.ihopkc.org.

Library of Congress Cataloging-in-Publication Data:
An application to register this book for cataloging has been submitted to the Library of Congress.
International Standard Book Number: 978-1-62999-576-2
E-book ISBN: 978-1-62999-577-9

Portions of this book were previously published by Charisma House as *Growing in Prayer*, ISBN 978-1-62136-046-9, copyright © 2014.

19 20 21 22 23 — 6 5 4 3 2
Printed in the United States of America

Introduction

VERY SIMPLY, PRAYER is "talking with God." And a consistent prayer life is something you want to cultivate or else you wouldn't have picked up this devotional.

Although most believers are aware that the Lord is calling them to grow in their prayer lives, somehow other things always seem to get in the way. The good news is that the Holy Spirit will help all of us who desire to pray more effectively. For our part, we must ask Him for help, put into practice the biblical principles related to prayer, and stick with the process, even when we feel as if it isn't working.

As a young man, I knew I needed to grow in prayer. I read books about prayer and revival, and knew my own prayer life was lacking. I wanted to experience the deep things of God, so I determined to spend an hour in prayer each night, even if it killed me. I referred to that hour of prayer as the hour of death because it was so boring. I exhausted everything I could think to pray about in two minutes. How in the world would I fill in the remaining fifty-eight minutes?

I had the idea that prayer was complicated, mysterious, and difficult, but on my journey of growing in prayer, I found that it is instead simple, immensely practical, and often very enjoyable. Prayer can take many forms, but all prayer is essentially a two-way conversation with the Lord that has real, life-changing results.

Enjoyable prayer is prayer that refreshes our hearts and invigorates our spirits. Imagine what it is like for prayer to be enjoyable! We will want to engage in it continually. Only enjoyable prayer is prayer that is sustainable. On the other hand, if it is not enjoyable, we will only pray intermittently—or not at all.

Being a person of prayer is the highest calling in one's life. Not every believer is called to preach, but *every* Christian is called to pray. Prayer is essential for our spiritual well-being. It is not an optional activity.

This book is not intended to be an exhaustive resource on prayer but rather a practical daily devotional to guide you into the foundational truths about prayer: why God ordained it, how we do it, how we grow in it, what it accomplishes, and so forth.

Don't rush through this book. Take each devotional *one day at a time*. Savor what you learn on each page and ask the Holy Spirit to help you apply the lessons to your life. Each devotional is followed by a corresponding scripture and a Prayer Starter to jump-start you on your new journey into the prayerful life.

Remember, when we pray we are not just reciting rote catechisms; we are communing with the Creator of the universe—the omnipotent One—who delights to hear from us and longs to share *life* with us.

Day 1

You Are Called to Pray

*As it is the business of tailors to mend
clothes and cobblers to make shoes, so it
is the business of Christians to pray.*

—MARTIN LUTHER

WE BEGIN OUR journey of growing in prayer (and intimacy with God) by acknowledging that prayer is not only for beginners but also for mature believers. Otherwise, there would be no point in trying to grow in it! The Lord calls *every* believer to a life of prayer— no matter how long he has been saved or how experienced he is in this discipline. The best thing all of us can do to improve ourselves, our lives, and our relationships is to grow in prayer.

Jesus made it clear that we cannot walk in the fullness of our destinies in God without growing in prayer. He said that unless we abide in Him, we can do nothing related to bearing fruit for His kingdom or maturing in our spiritual lives (John 15:5). How do we abide in Him? The core activity of abiding in Christ is prayer—simply talking to Jesus.

Because we are not the source of spiritual life ourselves, we cannot generate it, nor can we receive it unless we abide in Christ. Just as it is impossible for us to jump a hundred feet even if we push ourselves, it is impossible for us to generate spiritual life. It is not an issue of practice; we were not created to be able to jump a hundred feet! And neither were we created to have Spirit-life while living independently of the Spirit. We must abide in Christ and grow in prayer to make our lives work.

The Holy Spirit will move in a new and powerful way in your

heart and life as you take time to grow in prayer. The change may not happen overnight, but it will most certainly happen. The discipline of prayer will eventually become delight in prayer. Dryness in prayer will gradually be replaced by a vibrant dialogue with God that will change your life and result in many answered prayers.

I invite you to begin the next stage of your journey in prayer right now. There is no better time than today. Do not wait for a special spiritual experience to begin to grow in prayer. We grow in prayer by actually *praying*. Beginners in prayer mature simply by praying more. It is the same principle we embrace when learning to play a musical instrument—we become better the more we practice.

WHAT CAN I DO?

One step you can take that will help you grow in prayer is to set a schedule for regular prayer times. A schedule establishes *when* you will pray, and it will help you to be consistent in talking to Jesus. You must not limit your prayer life to your scheduled prayer time, and you may never keep more than 70 percent to 80 percent of your scheduled times of prayer. But I have found that I pray much more consistently if I block out time on my schedule that is devoted to spending time with Jesus.

FOR REFLECTION

"He who abides in Me, and I in him, bears much fruit; for without Me you can do nothing" (John 15:5).

> *Lord, forgive me for not realizing how essential prayer is to my spiritual growth and for not making it a priority in my life. Help me to set aside time daily for focused communication with You.*

_____

_____

_____

_____

_____

_____

_____

_____

_____

_____

_____

_____

_____

_____

_____

_____

_____

_____

_____

_____

_____

_____

_____

_____

_____

_____

_____

_____

_____

_____

Day 2

From Duty to Delight

He who has learned to pray has learned the
greatest secret of a holy and happy life.

—WILLIAM LAW

IN MY YOUNGER days I loved Jesus but dreaded spending time in prayer. I saw prayer as a necessary duty I had to endure if I wanted to receive more blessing.

In the summer of 1974 one of my youth leaders exhorted me to set aside an hour every day for prayer, and I determined to try. I was a freshman at the University of Missouri, living in a student apartment with three other believers. I told them, "I will pray an hour a day, even if it kills me." My announcement brought an element of accountability, knowing that each night they would watch me to see if I actually kept my commitment. So I set my prayer time from nine to ten each night. I referred to it as the "hour of death" because it was so boring I felt as if I was going to die.

At 9:00 p.m. I began my hour of prayer by mentioning everything I could think of to God. I exhausted my entire list in about two minutes: "Thank You, Jesus, for my health, for food, for my friends. Please help me score touchdowns on the university football team, and help me make good grades..." I looked at my watch, and I still had fifty-eight minutes to go! Some of those prayers were never answered. I did make the university football team, but I never made any touchdowns, and I made only average grades.

I endured that dreadful hour night after night. I did not like it at all. I enjoyed activities such as going to worship services and attending Bible studies to hear teaching. I liked engaging in ministry activity and going on missions trips. But when I got alone to pray or read the Bible, I found it confusing and boring. However, I really wanted to grow in God, so I knew I had to stick with this "prayer thing" until I developed a real life in prayer. I was determined—but not very hopeful that it would work for me.

My friend Larry Lea encouraged me by declaring that when we persist in prayer, our prayer life progresses from duty to discipline to delight. I was not sure how it would happen, but I fiercely resolved to find out. By the grace of God, it "worked."

To be successful, I needed a new perspective on prayer: I needed to know what prayer is and why the Lord insists on it. Isaiah prophesied that the Lord would make His servants joyful in His house of prayer (Isa. 56:7). Here Isaiah referred to a new paradigm for prayer: prayer characterized by joy. It is what I like to call "enjoyable prayer." The Lord desires that the church be surprised by joy in communicating with Him.

WHAT CAN I DO?

Start with a manageable amount of time set aside for prayer each day—maybe fifteen minutes—and stick to it. As you persist, ask the Holy Spirit to help you progress from duty to discipline to delight. Eventually your prayer time will increase as you are caught up in the delight of communing with your heavenly Father.

FOR REFLECTION

"I will bring [them] to My holy mountain, and make them joyful in My house of prayer" (Isa. 56:7).

> *Lord, I long to progress from duty to discipline unto delight as I spend time with You. Take me by the hand and lead me into Your house of prayer so that I may experience prayer that is*

enjoyable. Oh, that I may experience the joyful delight of communing with You today.

_____

_____

_____

_____

_____

_____

_____

_____

_____

_____

_____

_____

_____

_____

_____

_____

_____

_____

_____

_____

_____

_____

_____

_____

Day 3

A Place of Encounter

*Prayer should not be regarded as a duty
which must be performed, but rather as a
privilege to be enjoyed, a rare delight that
is always revealing some new beauty.*

—E. M. BOUNDS

FIRST AND FOREMOST, prayer is about encountering God and growing in relationship with Him. In prayer we position ourselves to receive fresh insight into His heart as new desires are formed in our hearts, enabling us to commune deeply with Him. Prayer positions us to be energized to love—to love God and people. Yes, it is biblical to pray to get answers and to see God's power. But prayer is first of all an opportunity to commune with God.

The call to prayer is a call to participate in the love that has forever burned in God's heart. From eternity past, the Father has loved the Son with all His heart, and the Son has loved the Father with the same intensity. This love is the foundational reality of the kingdom of God. It is this very reality that we participate in as we grow in prayer, and it is what prayer is mostly about—that is, participating in the family dynamics of the Godhead.

God created the human race to share His love. Why? Simply because "God is love" (1 John 4:16).

God's heart burns with love, and He calls us to experience it—to enter into what I refer to as "the fellowship of the burning heart." Salvation is an invitation to this fellowship.

WHAT CAN I DO?

As you pray today, actively position yourself to receive the love of God, and ask the Holy Spirit to draw you into the fellowship of the burning heart.

FOR REFLECTION

"And we have known and believed the love that God has for us. God is love, and he who abides in love abides in God, and God in him" (1 John 4:16).

> *Lord, I will seek daily prayer encounters with You, not only to strengthen our relationship but to partake of the abiding love that is only found when I am in Your presence.*

_____

_____

_____

_____

_____

_____

_____

_____

_____

_____

_____

_____

_____

_____

_____

Day 4

Prayer That Produces Results

*It is not enough to begin to pray...but
we must patiently, believingly continue in
prayer until we obtain an answer.*

—George Müller

WE DO NOT pray "just to pray." Yes, we pray to commune with God, but we also pray so that things will change and God's blessings will be released in us and through us. There is a point to our prayers. In the apostle James' teaching on prayer, he wrote of the power of prayer: "The effective, fervent prayer of a righteous man avails much" (James 5:16). Effective prayer accomplishes much and leads to real results. Jesus taught His disciples, saying, "If you ask anything in My name, I will do it" (John 14:14).

We are to pray in faith believing that God will answer them by releasing a greater measure of His blessing and power. Jesus often affirmed people who had faith to receive from Him. On the other hand, He rebuked those who could not receive because of their lack of faith in Him.

Matthew 17:14–21 recounts the story of the man who brought his epileptic son to the disciples to be healed but was disappointed because "they could not cure him." Publicly, Jesus expressed pain over the "faithless and perverse generation" and then healed the boy instantly. Later, in private, when the disciples asked why they could not drive the demon out of the boy, Jesus stated the reason simply and categorically: "Because of your unbelief." He added that nothing would be impossible for those who pray with faith. We are called to be channels of His blessing and healing to others. The disciples learned much from Jesus: when they prayed in faith and obedience, things changed. The same will be true of us.

WHAT CAN I DO?

Practice childlike faith as you pray to the Father today. And don't be afraid to say, "Lord, I believe. Help my unbelief!" He longs to draw you into the fellowship of the Trinity.

FOR REFLECTION

"Therefore I say to you, whatever things you ask when you pray, believe that you receive them, and you will have them" (Mark 11:24).

> *Lord, forgive me for not always trusting You to answer my prayers. I will believe in Your power to guide me in faith and provide results.*

Day 5

Prayer Unleashes Blessings

A glimpse of Jesus will save you. To gaze at Him will sanctify you.

—MANLEY BEASLEY

THE LORD LONGS to be gracious, to release a greater measure of His grace and blessing to us. He will surely do this at the sound of our cry—when He hears it, He will answer us. Receiving more from God is not about convincing Him to be willing to give us more. Rather, it is about God's convincing His people to pray for more with confidence.

Blessings are promised to those who come to God and ask. Therefore, if we pray, the quality of our natural and spiritual lives will improve. For example, the measure in which we receive insight from the Holy Spirit will increase, and our thirsty hearts will encounter God more deeply.

By praying, we can both release God's blessing in greater measure and cut off the work of the enemy, who seeks to devour our finances, break our bodies, ruin our relationships, oppress our hearts, and destroy our families. God opens doors of blessing and closes doors of oppression in response to prayer. When we pray, doors of demonic oppression can be shut. We have authority in Jesus' name to stop demonic activity and to release angelic activity in our lives and the lives of others.

God will not do our part, and we cannot do His part. God requires that we cooperate with Him according to His supernatural grace. This is an expression of His desire for intimate partnership with us. Only through a lifestyle of prayer can we receive the fullness of what God has promised.

WHAT CAN I DO?

Ask the Lord to open doors of blessing in your life and the lives of your loved ones in a greater measure. Ask Him to close doors of oppression so that demonic interference will be shut down.

FOR REFLECTION

"The LORD longs to be gracious to you, and therefore He waits on high to have compassion on you....He will surely be gracious to you at the sound of your cry; when He hears it, He will answer you" (Isa. 30:18–19, NASB).

> *Lord, grant me the ability to pray with great confidence. You are such a gracious God—always ready to respond to my cries. I seek to unleash Your blessings through prayer and receive them with a spirit of joy.*

Day 6

Prayer Is Partnership With God

*If you want that splendid power in prayer, you
must remain in loving, living, lasting, conscious,
practical, abiding union with the Lord Jesus Christ.*

—C. H. Spurgeon

THE LORD WANTS much more from His people than for them to
be His workforce. He longs to have relationship with those who
love Him and to partner with them in accomplishing His purposes.

When our two sons were little, God used a simple episode from
our family life to teach me about partnering in prayer with His
purposes. One day when I came home, my wife, Diane, was in the
kitchen with our son Luke, who was about five years old at the time.
They had just finished washing the dishes together. My son's shirt
was soaked with water. My wife's hair was damp and sticking up, and
there was a broken plate on the floor. Things were a little messy. I
asked, "What happened?"

Luke smiled and said with great pride, "Hey, Dad, I just washed
the dishes."

So Luke had made a big mess, broken a dish, and got water every-
where, yet in his mind he "washed the dishes." But he was happy, and
his big smile said, "Dad, look what I did—I washed the dishes."

In that moment I gained a new insight into how prayer works.
Diane could have washed the dishes much faster without Luke's
help, but she wanted to involve him. The Lord can easily build His
kingdom without using us, but He wants to involve us because He
is committed to a relationship of partnership with us. Jesus is not
just a King with power; He is also a Bridegroom with a desire for

relationship. He has joy in our friendship and in our partnering together in the work of the kingdom with Him.

WHAT CAN I DO?

Find out how you can bless the Lord today. Ask Him, "Lord, how can I be a blessing to You and to those You want to bless through me today?" Position yourself to listen for His response. It may come as a still, small voice, or it may come as an impression in the moment.

FOR REFLECTION

"Now may the God of peace who brought up our Lord Jesus from the dead...make you complete in every good work to do His will, working in you what is well pleasing in His sight, through Jesus Christ, to whom be glory forever and ever. Amen" (Heb. 13:20–21).

> *Lord, thank You for desiring a relationship with me. You are mighty and don't need my help, but Your longing for partnership with me exemplifies Your awesome love. I pray that I grow in my partnership with You.*

How can I be a blessing to you Lord today?

Day 7

The Importance of Asking

*It is in the process of being worshipped that
God communicates His presence to men.*

—C. S. Lewis

MOST OF US know the Bible verse that teaches that we have not because we ask not (James 4:2). God wants us to do more than simply *think* about our needs; He wants us to *ask* Him to meet them. Many complain about their lives or their circumstances and even talk to others about them, but they do not speak their needs out to the Lord.

It is easy to think about our needs without verbalizing them. Why does God insist on our asking? It is because the "asking" leads to a greater heart-connect with Him. Therefore, He "starves us out" of our prayer-less lives by withholding certain blessings until we ask—until we actually *talk* to Him about them. When the pressure caused by the lack of His blessing is greater than our busyness, then we pray more. And in the process of praying, we connect with Him relationally.

The Lord knows our needs without our asking, yet He waits to give us many things until we ask Him for them. Jesus called us to ask and keep on asking, to seek and keep on seeking, to knock and keep on knocking. The verbs in the Greek are in the continuous present tense, indicating that we are to do this consistently and keep on doing it. Asking is important.

WHAT CAN I DO?

Just ask. It sounds so simple, yet often we neglect to do it. As you go through your day, ask the Lord for answers to the burdens on your heart, or even in the simplest of things that you know you need His help in.

FOR REFLECTION

"Ask, and it will be given to you; seek, and you will find; knock, and it will be opened to you. For everyone who asks receives, and he who seeks finds, and to him who knocks it will be opened" (Matt. 7:7–8).

> *Lord, forgive me for not always coming to You with my needs. You alone can meet them, and yet I often do not turn to You first. Help me to talk to You consistently about my needs and continuously ask You to meet them.*

Day 8

Imperfect Prayers Still Move the Heart of God

You can do more than pray after you have prayed; but you cannot do more than pray until you have prayed.

—S. D. GORDON

OUR PRAYERS DON'T have to be expressed perfectly to accomplish God's purposes. They are effective because of the authority we have in Jesus, which is based on His finished work on the cross. Therefore, our prayers are effective even when they are *short*, when they are *weak*, and when they are *poorly worded*.

Short prayers are effective. Do not put off praying until you have a full hour to pray. Even while you are rushing to an appointment, waiting at a stoplight, or standing in line at a store, you can offer ninety-second prayers that will make a difference in your life and the lives of others. Likewise, do not measure your prayers by how you feel when you pray them but by the extent to which they agree with God's will and Word. Beloved, our weak prayer times may not move us, but they move the heart of God.

Finally, God values our prayers even when we do not say them in the "right" way. We sometimes think we must have perfect wording when we pray. But we come boldly to the "throne of grace" (Heb. 4:16), not the "throne of literary accuracy." The Lord hears the groan of the prisoner (Ps. 79:11; 102:20) as well as the eloquence of biblical scholars and powerful preachers. Remember, God knows our hearts—and He has given us His Spirit to intercede through us and for us.

WHAT CAN I DO?

Bring your short, weak, or poorly worded prayers before the Lord today. Present your petitions and devotions with the confidence you have in Jesus Christ.

FOR REFLECTION

"Now this is the confidence that we have in Him, that if we ask anything according to His will, He hears us" (1 John 5:14).

> *Lord, thank You for the knowledge that You hear my prayers even when they are weak, short, or poorly worded. My prayers may not always be eloquent, but You listen and respond to them regardless of my shortcomings.*

Day 9

Our Prayers Move Angels

Prayer does not fit us for the greater
works; prayer is the greater work.

—OSWALD CHAMBERS

IN JULY 1988 I had a life-changing encounter at a Saturday morning prayer meeting I had been leading for nearly four years. One Saturday I arrived around fifteen minutes early. The only two cars in the parking lot belonged to the young guys who were running the sound system.

As I approached the door to enter the building, I heard music that sounded like something from the "Hallelujah Chorus" in Handel's *Messiah*. It was glorious and beautiful and very loud. I thought, "Oh no, the sound techs are playing with the sound system, and they will surely blow out the speakers by having the volume up so loud." I ran to open the door and ask them to turn the volume down, but when I opened the door, everything was quiet. I thought, "What is going on?"

Inside the sanctuary, the only two guys there were not in the sound booth but rather at the front of the sanctuary praying together. I was perplexed until it dawned on me, with a sense of awe, that I had literally heard angelic choirs.

The prayer meeting began, and I thought that at any moment the glory of God would manifest in an unusual way. Surely hearing the angelic voices was a sign that we were about to witness a dramatic breakthrough of God's presence! But nothing of the sort happened. It was as run-of-the-mill as it was on many other Saturdays.

After the prayer meeting was over and everyone else had left the building, I sat quietly by myself and thought, "Hearing that angelic choir was one of the strangest things that has ever happened to me. What did it mean, Lord? Why didn't something dynamic happen today in the prayer meeting?"

Suddenly the Lord gave me a very clear word. It came as an impression. The Holy Spirit said, "This is what happens every time a few of My people gather to pray." I understood in that moment that angelic choirs rejoice every time God's people gather to pray, even in a small, seemingly uninspired or "unanointed" Saturday morning prayer meeting. Beloved, our private times of prayer and our public prayer meetings may not move us, but they move the angels, and more importantly, they move the heart of God.

WHAT CAN I DO?

Picture the heavenly host joining in as you spend time alone with God or pray with the corporate body in your church. Thank Him for what is taking place beyond the veil that separates the unseen spiritual world from the natural world.

FOR REFLECTION

"[While Cornelius was praying the angel] said to him, 'Your prayers and your alms have come up for a memorial before God'" (Acts 10:4).

Lord, it is wondrous to know that our prayers can actually move angels to sing! Going forward, I will try not to take my private or public moments of prayer for granted.

Day 10

The Fellowship of the Burning Heart

God does nothing but by prayer,
and everything with it.

—JOHN WESLEY

CONTRARY TO WHAT some people think, salvation is much more than a means of escaping hell. Salvation is also more than a means of gaining earthly happiness by receiving God's blessing on one's circumstances.

Jesus was after so much more than making our lives easy and comfortable when He died on the cross for us. There is something much bigger going on. We have been offered the great privilege of knowing God, and the call to grow in prayer is a call to participate in some of the family dynamics within the Godhead.

The love burning in God's heart has at least five expressions: 1) God loves God (the Trinity) with a fiery love; 2) God loves His people; 3) our love for God springs from His love imparted to us; 4) God's people love themselves in God's love and for God's sake; and 5) God's people love one another in the overflow of the love we receive from God. Together these five expressions of love constitute "the fellowship of the burning heart." We are invited to enter into the relationship of burning love that is shared within the fellowship of the Trinity. What a glorious destiny!

WHAT CAN I DO?

When you pray today, ask the Lord to open your eyes to the "bigger picture" going on and to fill you with His love for people.

FOR REFLECTION

"This is eternal life, that they may know You, the only true God, and Jesus Christ" (John 17:3).

> *Lord, thank You for the awesome opportunity as a believer to join in Your "fellowship of the burning heart." The chance to commune with You through prayer is such a great privilege. Help me to recognize these five expressions and grow in understanding them as a real part of my prayer life.*

Day 11

Gazing on God's Beauty

*Worship changes the worshiper into
the image of the One worshiped.*

—JACK HAYFORD

GOD CREATED HUMAN beings in such a way that we crave fascination, wonder, and awe, and our craving is best fulfilled by beholding God's beauty—the beauty that He possesses in Himself and expresses in creation. King David understood this truth so well that he declared beholding God's beauty was the solitary goal of his prayer life.

By fellowshipping with Jesus, we are connecting with the Man who is ultimate beauty (Ps. 27:4). Therefore, as we grow in prayer, our capacity to enjoy beauty increases. Seeing the beauty of Jesus' person enables us to more clearly see His beauty in creation and redemption, and His leadership of history. It also works the other way around. Seeing Jesus' beauty through Scripture, nature, and His sovereign leadership over the church, the nations, and history helps us to see the beauty of His person.

The many facets of God's beauty are summed up in one reality—wholehearted *love*. Our lifelong search is really the search for deep relationship, lasting purpose, delight, and beauty. Our search ends not in things but in a person—in God's presence. The Russian novelist Dostoyevsky wrote that "to live without God is nothing but torture."[1]

Our hearts thirst for the eternal, for transcendence, and they can be filled only by participating in the fellowship of the burning heart with the Father, Son, and Holy Spirit.

WHAT CAN I DO?

Using a Bible concordance or Bible app, do a search for *beauty* or *beauty of holiness* to see what the Word has to say about God's beauty. Focus on His glory and beauty as you go about your business today.

FOR REFLECTION

"One thing I have desired of the LORD, that will I seek...to behold the beauty of the LORD" (Ps. 27:4).

> *Lord, Your magnificence is revealed throughout Scripture, history, and creation! I will revel in Your beauty as I go about my day and fellowship with You through daily prayer or simple communion with You.*

_____

_____

_____

_____

_____

_____

_____

_____

_____

_____

_____

_____

_____

Day 12

The Divine Cure for Boredom

You have made us for yourself, O Lord, and
our hearts are restless until they rest in You.

—St. Augustine

THE WORST TRAGEDY in life is to live in continual boredom without interacting with the divine. Bored people are compelled to search for different pleasures to fill their spiritual emptiness and loneliness. If we are not growing in our understanding of the beauty of Jesus and His purpose, then we will inevitably spend our free time and resources seeking fame, fortune, pleasure, entertainment, and recognition from others. They may temporarily deaden the pain of emptiness and loneliness, which stems from not having a growing relationship with God, but encountering beauty is the only real and lasting solution to overcoming boredom.

We will never be completely satisfied by our achievements, skills, wealth, fame, pleasures, or possessions. Why? Because the human heart was created to need more than what is available to us in the natural realm. Only the eternal, supernatural God can fill our longings. We are created by God's design to need deep connection with Him for our deepest longing to be satisfied.

Saint Augustine prayed: "You have made us for yourself, O Lord, and our hearts are restless until they rest in You."[1]

Human beings are unique in all of creation in that we are satisfied only by becoming more than what our human nature defines. We are spiritual beings who need something beyond what we received in our natural makeup. This "something" is best found in our interaction with God, who is ultimate beauty—thus, through prayer. The more

25

we grow in prayer, the more we will have the capacity to enjoy God's beauty as we were created to.

WHAT CAN I DO?

If you find yourself with empty time today, fill it with prayer, reading the Word, or simply meditating on God and His goodness. Notice how that "divine time" impacts the rest of your day.

FOR REFLECTION

"May the grace of the Lord Jesus Christ, and the love of God, and the fellowship of the Holy Spirit be with you all" (2 Cor. 13:14).

> *Father, help me to turn away from earthly pursuits that have the illusion of satisfying me in the moment but only leave me with feelings of emptiness. Only You can meet my heart's longing for more.*

_____

_____

_____

_____

_____

_____

_____

_____

_____

_____

_____

_____

Day 13

What Makes a Prayer Effective?

*The great people of the earth today are the people
who pray. I do not mean those who talk about
prayer; not those who can explain about prayer;
but I mean those people who take time and pray.*

—S. D. GORDON

THE APOSTLE JAMES, who was known in the early church as a great
man of prayer, gave the church invaluable insight into the sub-
ject of prayer that actually makes a difference and accomplishes its
intended goal.

God calls us to offer holy, believing, persevering prayer that flows
from relationship with the Lord and His family—this is the kind of
prayer that accomplishes much.

It is the destiny of every believer to release the power of God
through his simple prayers. James 5:15–16 says that the prayer of
faith will deliver the sick and that our prayers can avail (accomplish)
much. Our prayers accomplish much more than we can gauge with
our five senses, and the reality that they bring real change gives our
lives and our prayers great value. Our perspective on life changes dramatically when we believe that our prayers really make a difference.

The effective prayer James wrote about has four characteristics:
prayer *rooted in faith;* prayer in the *context of good relationships;*
prayer from a *lifestyle of righteousness;* and prayer that is *earnest.*
Amazing, isn't it, how a prayer can be both simple and powerful at
the same time?

WHAT CAN I DO?

As you pray today, believe that your prayers are making a difference. Then posture yourself to receive answers in God's timing.

FOR REFLECTION

"And the prayer of faith will save the sick, and the Lord will raise him up....Confess your trespasses to one another, and pray for one another, that you may be healed. The effective, fervent prayer of a righteous man avails much" (James 5:15–16).

> *Lord, I come before You rooted in faith, in right standing with my fellow believers, from a lifestyle of righteousness, and with an earnest heart. I know the prayers I pray today will accomplish far more than I can perceive with my five senses. Would You increase my faith today?*

_____

_____

_____

_____

_____

_____

_____

_____

_____

_____

_____

_____

_____

_____

Day 14

Prayer Rooted in Faith

*God does nothing except in
response to believing prayer.*

—John Wesley

THE PRAYER OF faith mentioned in James 5:15 is rooted in a three-fold confidence in God. First, it is prayer with confidence in the authority of Jesus over sickness and the works of darkness. Jesus affirmed a Roman centurion for having great faith in His authority over sickness (Matt. 8:5–13), and He told two blind men, "According to your faith let it be to you" (Matt. 9:29). Jesus strongly emphasized the importance of praying with faith or confidence (Mark 11:22–24). He also declared, "All authority has been given to Me in heaven and on earth" (Matt. 28:18). Our faith is to be anchored in the knowledge of His authority over every other power that exists.

Second, it is prayer with confidence in the blood of Jesus that qualifies weak people such as us to be vessels that release God's power and receive His blessings. In Hebrews we learn that we have "boldness to enter the Holiest by the blood of Jesus" (Heb. 10:19). We are not to shrink back due to shame or guilt, for He has given His own righteousness to us as a free gift (2 Cor. 5:21).

Third, it is prayer with confidence in the Father's desire to heal, set free, and bless His people by the work of the Holy Spirit. In Luke 11 Jesus concluded His teaching on prayer, saying, "If a son asks for bread from any father among you, will he give him a stone? Or if he asks for a fish, will he give him a serpent instead of a fish?...If you then, being evil, know how to give good gifts to your children, how much more will your heavenly Father give the Holy Spirit to those who ask Him!" (vv. 11–13). We pray in faith, knowing that God, whose heart burns with passion for us, really does desire to bless us.

WHAT CAN I DO?

Be bold as you talk to God. Pray "as if," just as Abraham "against all hope...in hope believed" (Rom. 4:18). Remember, you have confidence through the shed blood of Jesus Christ.

FOR REFLECTION

"For assuredly, I say to you, whoever says to this mountain, 'Be removed and be cast into the sea,' and does not doubt in his heart, but believes that those things he says will be done, he will have whatever he says" (Mark 11:23).

Father, I'm learning to pray with boldness and faith, believing that You not only hear but desire to answer my prayers according to Your will.

Day 15

The Importance of Good Relationships

*Talking to men about God is a great thing, but
talking to God about men is greater still.*

—E. M. BOUNDS

SOME BELIEVERS ARE committed to growing in relationship with others but are content to have a weak prayer life. Others are committed to growing in their prayer lives but are content to have weak relationships. The Bible sets these two values together as complementary, not competing.

They are not to be separated, because effective prayer flows best from those who are in strong kingdom relationships—sharing deeply with one another, partnering together in kingdom activities, and relating to one another in humility, honor, and forgiveness in the grace of God. Paul admonishes us in Colossians to "put on tender *mercies,* kindness, humility, meekness, longsuffering; bearing with one another, and forgiving one another." Then he adds, "But above all these things put on love, which is the bond of perfection" (Col. 3:12–14).

A strong prayer life will eventually lead to strong relationships with people. Those who sincerely value their relationship with Jesus are energized to love people more deeply. Prayer is not about being anti-relational or antisocial. True prayer has the opposite effect. It is all about love—loving God and people. People of prayer should be the most energized in love.

WHAT CAN I DO?

Allow the energizing love of the Holy Spirit to permeate your entire being, then go out and give that love away to others—even the ones who are hard to love and might not seem to want it.

FOR REFLECTION

"A new commandment I give to you, that you love one another; as I have loved you, that you also love one another. By this all will know that you are My disciples, if you have love for one another" (John 13:34–35).

Father, let my love for You—and time spent with You—spill over into my earthly relationships. Teach me by the Spirit to be more relatable, more loving, more kind and merciful to the people that I interact with today.

_____

_____

_____

_____

_____

_____

_____

_____

_____

_____

_____

_____

Day 16

A Lifestyle of Righteousness

*I have no such business I cannot get on without
spending three hours daily in prayer.*

—Martin Luther

A VERY IMPORTANT CONDITION for effectual prayer is to be committed to walking out a lifestyle of righteousness before God and people, as indicated in James 5:16: "The effective...prayer of a *righteous* man avails much." This biblical condition is often minimized or totally ignored, even by some who are deeply involved in the prayer-and-worship movement today.

The "righteous man" in this passage is any believer who sets his heart to obey Jesus as he seeks to walk in godly character with a lifestyle of practicing the truth (1 John 1:6). Setting our hearts to obey is very important, even if we fall short of mature, consistent obedience.

I have never met a person who is so mature in righteousness that he is above all temptation and never falls short in his walk with God. In other words, the prayers of a "righteous person" include the prayers of imperfect, weak people—such as you and me—who sincerely seek to walk in righteousness even as we stumble in our weakness. I am so grateful for the glorious reality of the grace of God!

WHAT CAN I DO?

Set your heart to obey Jesus and practice this truth in every facet of your life: your relationships, your finances, your speech, your thoughts, your actions, etc.

FOR REFLECTION

"Whatever we ask we receive from Him, because we keep His commandments and do those things that are pleasing in His sight" (1 John 3:22).

Father, though I am imperfect and weak, I sincerely seek to walk in righteousness. Give me a hunger and thirst for righteousness.

Day 17

Are Your Prayers Earnest?

Prayer will make a man cease from sin, or
sin will entice a man to cease from prayer.

—JOHN BUNYAN

USING THE PROPHET Elijah as an example, the apostle James taught that one characteristic of effective prayer is *earnestness* in prayer: "Elijah...prayed earnestly that it would not rain; and it did not rain" (James 5:17). What does it mean to be earnest?

First, earnest prayer comes from a heart that is engaged with God. To be earnest implies that we are not praying by rote or just going through the motions. Being earnest is the opposite of speaking our prayers mindlessly into the air. We are to focus our minds and attention toward the Lord when we pray.

Second, earnest prayer is prayer that is persistent. We must refuse to be denied answers to prayers that are in agreement with God's will. We must never stop asking and thanking God for the answers to prayers that are offered in His will until we see them with our eyes. We must not be casual about our prayer requests but persistent and tenacious.

Jesus taught a parable about the Father's willingness to answer prayer that is recorded in the Gospel of Luke. His message was that because of our persistence, the Father answers. He applied the parable by exhorting us to ask, knowing that the request will be fulfilled; to seek, knowing that we will find; and to knock, knowing that the door will open (Luke 11:9). The Greek verbs for "ask," "seek," and "knock" are in the continuous present tense. In other words, we are to ask and keep on asking, seek and keep on seeking, knock and keep on knocking. The message is a call to perseverance!

WHAT CAN I DO?

Refuse to give up on those "difficult" requests in your prayer time—some of those requests that you may have stopped praying for. Remember that some answers may be delayed for a reason only God knows. We can trust His leadership.

FOR REFLECTION

"Praying always with all prayer and supplication in the Spirit, being watchful to this end with all perseverance and supplication for all the saints" (Eph. 6:18).

> *Lord, I am asking You today for that same request I've presented before. I am asking, seeking, and knocking and won't stop until I hear from You on the matter.*

Day 18

Passion Does Not Equal Volume

*There is not a kind of life more sweet and delightful
than that of a continual conversation with God.*

—Brother Lawrence

A LLOW ME TO make a pastoral observation. During many years of leading in prayer, I have come across numerous people who devalue their prayers because they feel the prayers are not offered with enough emotion and energy. They misunderstand the nature of passionate or earnest prayer. It is mostly about being persistent and engaging with God from the heart. It is not about our prayer style in a public prayer meeting. But some conclude that they lack the necessary "passion" for God to answer their prayers because they don't express themselves with the same emotion or volume as those who lead out in public prayer.

The majority of us do not speak our prayers with intense emotion and volume in public, but we should not conclude that our prayers are ineffectual or second-class. If shouting is what defines earnest prayer, then about 99 percent of our prayers would be classed as non-passionate and lacking earnestness. Why? Because most of our prayers are offered as whispers from our hearts throughout the day. Even the most energetic prayer warriors probably offer less than 1 percent of their prayers in a public prayer meeting where they shout their prayers. Yet their private prayers, which are often mere whispers of the heart, are still earnest prayers. Quiet prayers can be passionate and earnest.

Passion is not about energy and volume; it is about being engaged from the heart with the Lord while praying and persevering in faith without quitting. So keep at it, and do not draw back, even if your prayer style is softer than that of others.

WHAT CAN I DO?

Keep whispering prayers to the Lord as you go about your day. Try not to gauge your prayers on the tone of your voice or by what you're feeling in the moment. No matter how weak your prayers may sound, they are real around the very corridors of the throne room! And remember that He hears even the faintest inward cry of the heart.

FOR REFLECTION

"Now Hannah spoke in her heart; only her lips moved, but her voice was not heard.... 'For this child I prayed, and the LORD has granted me my petition which I asked of Him'" (1 Sam. 1:13, 27).

> *Lord, it's good to know I don't have to shout and work up a sweat to be passionate in my devotion to You. Thank You that I can commune with You in a calm and peaceful way. Either way, I know You hear the cry of my heart.*

_____

_____

_____

_____

_____

_____

_____

_____

_____

_____

Day 19

Being Earnest Does Not Depend on "Feeling"

I live in prayer. I pray as I walk and when I lie down and arise. And the answers are always coming.

—George Müller

SOME DRAW BACK in their prayer lives because they embrace another wrong idea about earnest or fervent prayer. They believe they must *feel* God's presence when they pray. Thus, when they are discouraged or tired, they assume their prayers will be of no effect, and they stop praying. I have good news—our prayers are effective even when we are tired, discouraged, or not in a good mood. Remember that we offer our prayers to the Lord, who is always in a good mood and is never tired. We don't have to be happy and energetic for our prayers to be earnest and to avail much.

The work of the kingdom is based on who Jesus is and what He did on the cross, not on how we feel. God answers our prayers because of the blood of Jesus and His desire to partner with His people. If we measure ourselves by a wrong idea of what passion or being earnest in prayer is, then we will be tempted to pray much less.

Prayer is not about informing or persuading God but about connecting with Him in relationship. He is looking for conversation and dialogue with us. Some believers think that by praying more they *earn* the answers to their prayers. The Lord wants to converse with us far more than we want to talk with Him. We do not earn answers to prayers by our persistence or obedience.

WHAT CAN I DO?

Try flipping the script on this one: set yourself to "pray without ceasing" today (which includes unspoken prayers and whispers of the heart) regardless of how you feel. In fact, expect that you won't feel anything—but pray anyway. When you pray, remember that it's not in your repetition that you are heard nor in the eloquence of your speech but rather in your heart posture before Him.

FOR REFLECTION

"For the Lord GOD, the Holy One of Israel has said this, 'In returning [to Me] and rest you shall be saved, in quietness and confident trust is your strength'" (Isa. 30:15, AMP).

Lord, when I don't "feel" like praying, or feel Your presence when I pray, it's good to know that You are still present and well able to accomplish Your will.

_____

_____

_____

_____

_____

_____

_____

_____

_____

_____

_____

Weak People Can Pray Earnestly

*The one concern of the Devil is to keep us
from praying....He laughs at our toil, mocks
our wisdom, but he trembles when we pray.*

—SAMUEL CHADWICK

THE STORY OF Elijah is the story not of a great prophet of God but of the great God of the prophet. We may be surprised when we meet Elijah in the age to come. We may picture him as physically strong, with a dynamic personality, something like Charlton Heston when he played Moses in the famous movie *The Ten Commandments*. But he may, in fact, have been a physically weak and unimpressive man according to human standards. When we meet the great men and women of the Bible face to face, we may be surprised to discover just how much like us they are. It is faith in a great God that makes a great man or woman of God.

During the reign of King Ahab, Elijah called the people of Israel to repent of their backsliding. His prayers led to the healing of a nation when Israel turned back to God. Elijah prayed for a drought, and a drought came. Then three and a half years later, he prayed for rain to fall and break the drought. He prayed earnestly, with persistence. Seven times he prayed for the drought to break and the rains to come. Even though the Lord had told Elijah that He would send rain and had commanded Elijah to tell Ahab that rain was coming, the Lord required Elijah to pray until the rain actually came.

Elijah was a weak man with a nature like ours. He was prone to fear and discouragement, and he had the same weaknesses and temptations we face. Yet his prayer life was still very effective (1 Kings 17–19).

WHAT CAN I DO?

Acknowledge that you are a weak, imperfect person, like Elijah. Make that your starting point, and then lean in to what God wants to do, as He desires to commune with you and make Himself strong in your weakness.

FOR REFLECTION

"Elijah was a man with a nature like ours, and he prayed earnestly that it would not rain; and it did not rain...for three years and six months. And he prayed again, and the heaven gave rain" (James 5:17–18).

> *Lord, sometimes I am filled with fear and discouragement, just like Elijah. Thank You for using him to remind me that You work through weak and flawed people.*

_____

_____

_____

_____

_____

_____

_____

_____

_____

_____

Day 21

Our Prayers "Live" in God's Heart

Without worship, we go about miserable.

—A. W. TOZER

JAMES ASSURED US that much can be accomplished through the prayers of a righteous man (James 5:16). Indeed, our prayers accomplish much in this age *and* in the age to come.

In Revelation 5 we learn that all the prayers prayed in God's will throughout history are stored in golden bowls near the throne: "The twenty-four elders fell down before the Lamb, each having a harp, and golden bowls full of incense, which are the prayers of the saints" (Rev. 5:8; see also Rev. 8:1–6). Notice that the bowls will one day be "full." The fact that the bowls of prayer in heaven fill up implies that God does not forget our prayers. He still remembers our prayers from five years ago or even twenty years ago. We may have forgotten them, but God has not. They are in a golden bowl near to His throne and near to His heart.

Our prayers avail so much that they remain effective, or "alive," in God's sight long after this life, and I assume that they "live" forever in God's heart. Even the prayers from the distant past—from three hundred years ago or three thousand years ago—are still effective in God's presence. I believe that the prayers we offer today will still be effective in the distant future—five hundred or five thousand years from now. What we accomplish in prayer affects events on the earth today and also those in the distant future. As we gain greater understanding that our weak, simple prayers are not forgotten, we are motivated to persevere in prayer, even when we feel discouraged.

WHAT CAN I DO?

Be mindful that your prayers are being stored up in heaven in sacred bowls that are alive in God's sight, not just today, but for all eternity. Let this awareness fuel a new passion to pray, knowing that your prayers will be answered—that it's not a matter of *if* but *when*.

FOR REFLECTION

"Then another angel, having a golden censer, came and stood at the altar. He was given much incense, that he should offer it with the prayers of all the saints upon the golden altar which was before the throne" (Rev. 8:3).

> *Father, what a joy it is to know that all my prayers "live" before You in eternity. Nothing can blot them out!*

_____

_____

_____

_____

_____

_____

_____

_____

_____

_____

_____

_____

Day 22

"Abide in Me" Means "Talk to Me"

*The battle of prayer is against two things in
the earthlies: wandering thoughts, and lack of
intimacy with God....Neither can be cured
at once, but they can be cured by discipline.*

—Oswald Chambers

WHILE ON EARTH Jesus taught us how to live in dynamic union
with God. He declared that He is the vine, the source of life,
and that we are the branches, the expression of His life. In this
statement Jesus gave us one of His primary exhortations on living a
kingdom lifestyle, which is to "abide in Christ" so that we may bear
fruit that remains forever.

We bear fruit in two ways: inwardly in our character and outwardly in our ministry and service to others. Abiding in Christ is
one of the most neglected activities in the kingdom, yet it involves
only three simple aspects—talking to Jesus, applying His promises,
and obeying His leadership. These activities overlap, but they are not
the same.

The core task of abiding in Christ is talking to Jesus. It is so
simple that anyone can do it but so simple that many do not do it. I
often exchange the phrase "abide in Me" for the phrase "talk to Me."
Jesus has much to say to us, but He allows us to set the pace of the
conversation. If we start, He will continue the conversation as long as
we do. When we stop, He stops and waits until we begin again. He
responds in the degree to which we communicate with Him.

WHAT CAN I DO?

Keep the phrase "Talk to me" in your spirit as you go about your day today. Keep your spiritual ears open for whispers from the Spirit and make a point to respond with silent or vocal worship and a heart of gratitude.

FOR REFLECTION

"I am the vine, you are the branches. He who abides in Me, and I in him, bears much fruit....I chose you and appointed you that you should go and bear fruit, and that your fruit should remain" (John 15:5, 16).

> *Lord, thank You for making prayer so simple. I don't have to work myself up or speak with eloquent words. All I need to do is talk to You.*

_____

_____

_____

_____

_____

_____

_____

_____

_____

_____

Day 23

Applying His Promises

*I would rather teach one man to
pray than ten men to preach.*

—CHARLES SPURGEON

A SECOND ASPECT INVOLVED in abiding in Christ is applying the promises in His Word to our hearts. Emotions such as shame, guilt, fear, or rejection often rise up to challenge what God says in His Word about His loving us, forgiving us, and providing for us. The enemy challenges these truths in the Word and accuses God continually (Rev. 12:10).

We take a stand for what the Word says is true about us by speaking the Word over the negative emotions that rise up within us. The lies will not go away by themselves; they must be actively resisted as we confess the truths of the Word.

Many believers are still living under the tyranny of Satan's lies twenty or thirty years after they have been born again, believing their lives are worthless and that God has forgotten or rejected them. Others choose to ride out the storm of the negative emotions that rise up within them. But there is great power in the Word, and we must not neglect to apply His promises in the face of fear, condemnation, or other negative emotions. We can stand with confidence in God's sight because Jesus paid the price for our sin and took our condemnation.

WHAT CAN I DO?

Every time a negative or condemning thought enters your mind, counter it immediately with a promise from Scripture that declares the opposite, the God view of the matter. For instance, instead of seeing myself from a shame-based place—as a condemned failure who seems to not change fast enough—I speak the words "I am loved and am freely accepted by God since I have received the gift of righteousness through Christ."

FOR REFLECTION

"There is therefore now no condemnation for those who are in Christ Jesus" (Rom. 8:1).

> *Lord, today I speak the Word over the negative emotions that rise up within me. I stand before You with confidence because of Jesus Christ.*

Day 24

Obeying His Leadership

*He who has learned to pray has learned the
greatest secret of a holy and happy life.*

—S. D. GORDON

IN REVIEW, THE first aspect involved in abiding in Christ is to talk
to Jesus, and the second aspect is to apply God's promise to our life.
Here, the third aspect related to abiding in Christ is obeying His
leadership, and we must not minimize this vital part of abiding. Jesus
clearly stated that our obedience and our love for Him are closely
connected. (See John 14:21–23.)

It is popular today to minimize obedience in the name of mag-
nifying God's grace. Some preach a distorted grace message that
emphasizes the freedom of being forgiven while undermining the
necessity of loving Jesus in a spirit of obedience. But the biblical
grace message never minimizes obedience. God's wholehearted love
for us always calls for a response of our wholehearted love for Him,
as evidenced by our seeking to walk in obedience to Him.

The Bible tells us that it is the obedient, or the pure in heart, who
will see God (Matt. 5:8). What this means is that they will experience God more. The result of walking in purity is that our spiritual
capacity to feel or experience the love of God increases.

In summary, abiding in Christ involves three aspects—talking
with God, applying His promises, and obeying His leadership. Some
talk to Jesus regularly yet do not apply His Word to their hearts.
Others apply the Word but neglect to talk to Jesus regularly. Some
seek to obey Him but do not apply His Word. Others claim His
promises but do not set their hearts to obey Him. Abiding in Christ

requires *all three* of these activities, and it results in God's people being empowered to bear fruit that remains and to live a transformed life.

WHAT CAN I DO?

By now you may be getting better at attuning your spirit for the whispers of the still, small voice of God. As you sense His promptings, be quick to obey what He's leading you to do.

FOR REFLECTION

"He who has My commandments and keeps them, it is he who loves Me...I will love him and manifest Myself to him...If anyone loves Me, he will keep My word; and My Father will love him, and We will come to him and make Our home with him" (John 14:21–23).

> *Lord, help me today to abide in You—to talk with You, apply Your promises, and obey Your leadership. As I hide myself in You, so I will abide in You.*

Day 25

A Transforming Union— Christ in Us

If I could hear Christ praying for me in the next room, I would not fear a million enemies. Yet distance makes no difference. He is praying for me.

—ROBERT MURRAY MCCHEYNE

JESUS SPOKE IN detail about our union with God, which leads to our transformation. We see two elements of this transforming union in John 15:1–11—we abide in Christ, and Christ abides in us. The first idea, that our life is in Christ, is familiar to most of us, but the truth that Christ lives in us is often overlooked.

Christ abides—lives—in our spirits *instantly* when we are born again, and He abides in our hearts *progressively* as He manifests His presence in our minds and emotions. In John 15 Jesus was referring to this second aspect of abiding. The apostle Paul prayed that Jesus would abide, or dwell, in the Ephesian believers' hearts. He also wrote of Christ's being formed in our hearts (Gal. 4:19). The Holy Spirit wants to form Jesus in our hearts—in other words, in our personalities.

Many know the verse, "Behold, I stand at the door and knock" (Rev. 3:20). Jesus is presented as knocking at the doors of hearts, and we often use this verse with unbelievers. We ask them, "Do you want to invite Jesus into your heart?" But written as it was to the church of Laodicea, this verse is primarily addressing believers. Jesus wanted deeper fellowship with them and desired to move in their lives in a greater way as they opened the doors of their hearts to Him. During

His earthly ministry, Jesus promised that the Holy Spirit would flow like a river out of the hearts of His people to inspire, direct, and transform their minds and emotions, and to minister in power through them to others!

WHAT CAN I DO?

Jesus desires deeper fellowship with you, so seek to lean into His heart today by just talking to Him softly in the midst of your daily tasks or assignments. Every time Jesus knocks at the door of your heart—essentially saying, "Let's spend time together"—respond with a yes. Even if you're at work or busy with some essential task, talk to Him internally and "worship" silently. You'll never get those moments back, so make them count.

FOR REFLECTION

"...that He [Jesus] would grant you, according to the riches of His glory, to be strengthened with might through His Spirit in the inner man, that Christ may dwell in your hearts through faith" (Eph. 3:16–17).

> *Lord, manifest Your presence more and more in my heart so that the Holy Spirit will flow like a river out of me into those around me. Give me a nudge when I'm too busy or distracted. Remind me that it's time to connect with You again.*

Day 26

Getting Practical

*Don't pray when you feel like it. Have an
appointment with the King and keep it.*

—Corrie ten Boom

I UNDERSTAND THE DIFFICULTIES you may experience in developing a consistent prayer life because I too have struggled through many of the same difficulties. But by the grace of God, I have been able to maintain a consistent prayer life for more than thirty-five years. My advice: have a prayer plan. Here's the three-part plan that I still use today:

- Set a schedule for regular prayer times. A schedule establishes *when* you will pray.

- Make a prayer list. A prayer list helps you to focus on *what* to pray.

- Cultivate a right view of God. A right view of God causes you to *want* to pray.

If you will embrace these three simple steps, over time both your consistency and enjoyment of prayer will increase dramatically. When I was struggling in college to establish my prayer life, a leader suggested that I schedule a time each day and make a prayer list. He assured me that doing these two things would change my prayer life over time. He was right! I was hesitant at first, but his counsel to me worked.

If you schedule time for prayer and make a prayer list, you will pray ten times more than you do now. I have made this statement for more than thirty years. People usually do not believe it, and some even argue against it. Nevertheless, I am sticking by it because I have proved the truth of it in my own life and witnessed the results of others' applying the plan in their lives. It will work for you too. Some of you will wonder why you did not start this practice much sooner!

WHAT CAN I DO?

Create a prayer journal to write down your petitions and thoughts about whatever is going on in your life. Be sure to date your prayers. Then, six months later, look back to see how many of your requests have been answered.

FOR REFLECTION

"Yet regard the prayer of Your servant and his supplication, O LORD my God, and listen to the cry and the prayer which Your servant is praying before You" (2 Chron. 6:19).

> *Lord, I've struggled with consistent prayer in the past and sometimes even avoided it. But with Your help I am learning to see that "prayer without ceasing" is like breathing. Thank You for showing me that I can do this. Help me to implement this in my life. I pray for grace to sign up for it over and over again, knowing that even if I fall short, I can still have a yes in my heart for tomorrow.*

Day 27

Discipline Is Not Legalism

*We have to pray with our eyes on
God, not on the difficulties.*

—OSWALD CHAMBERS

SOME PEOPLE PROTEST that it is legalistic to schedule time for prayer or use a prayer list. It can be, but it does not have to be. We step into legalism when we seek to earn God's love by praying or obeying rules. The good news of the gospel is that we don't have to earn it; God offers His love and grace freely. Consistency in prayer—talking to the Lord regularly and with focus—simply positions us to sit before Him more often so that we can experience more of His free grace daily.

Setting a regular time for prayer is not an attempt to earn God's love; it is a reflection of our desire to take control of our schedules so that we can make prayer a priority. I urge you not to fall for the age-old lie that automatically calls all discipline "legalism." This lie has robbed many of the blessing of a consistent prayer life. Being aimless or passive and thinking only of the present moment is not what liberty in grace is about.

God's grace empowers us to discipline our time, money, and appetites in a way that fulfills His will for our lives, positions us to experience more of His grace, and enables us to encounter Him in a greater way. What Jesus freely offers in grace and what we actually experience are often two very different things. I want to practically experience in my everyday life all He freely offers me! I am able to best do this as I make it a priority to talk to Him. Scheduling time for Him is an expression of both my love for Him and my hunger for more.

WHAT CAN I DO?

Schedule a regular daily prayer time and be realistic with yourself. If you struggle with mornings, maybe pray at night instead. If you are a nature person, consider talking to God as you walk outside. Be creative.

FOR REFLECTION

"For you, brethren, have been called to liberty; only do not use liberty as an opportunity for the flesh" (Gal. 5:13).

> *Father, Your grace overwhelms me. Thank You that what You freely offer in grace I can actually experience in my life. I pray that You would set me free from any bonds of legalism in my own life and that You would open my eyes to Your beauty and show me different ways that I can express my love for You.*

Day 28

Loving Our Heavenly Father

A life growing in its purity and devotion
will be a more prayerful life.

—E. M. BOUNDS

MY EARTHLY FATHER and I were good friends. He was my number one cheerleader, and during my childhood he affirmed me consistently. There was no one I liked being around more than my dad. I liked being with him because I knew he enjoyed being with me, and I felt it.

I remember when I first discovered that the Lord likes me even more than my dad did. When I saw that truth, I wanted to be with the Lord and talk to Him much more than I had desired to before. It is enjoyable to talk to someone who really likes you!

Just before Jesus died, He made an astounding request of His Father. He asked "that the world may know that You [the Father]...have loved them [God's people] as You have loved Me [Jesus]" (John 17:23). Jesus wants us to know that His Father loves us just as He loves Jesus! Jesus' prayer gives us insight into the great value we have in God's eyes. The revelation that the Father loves us as He loves Jesus is a profound statement of our worth to Him.

Paul tells us that we have "received the Spirit of adoption by whom we cry out, 'Abba, Father'" (Rom. 8:15). In Hebrew *Abba* is a term of endearment for a father, much like "Papa" in our culture; it indicates respect but also affection and intimacy. The understanding of God as "Abba" and the knowledge of our identity as His adopted children equip us to reject Satan's accusations that we are hopeless failures.

This truth, that Abba-God enjoys us even in our weakness, is a stabilizing anchor that gives us confidence in prayer. As sons and daughters of God we are able to approach His throne with confidence and without shame or hesitation.

WHAT CAN I DO?

Practice calling God "Abba" in your prayer times and even as you converse with Him throughout the day. Just vocalizing that word on a regular basis will cause you to see Him in a different light and realize how He sees you—as His son or daughter. Look for passages in the Bible that talk about God being "our Father" and ask the Holy Spirit to begin to give you more insight into God's role as Father in your life.

FOR REFLECTION

"The LORD delights in you...and as the bridegroom rejoices over the bride, so shall your God rejoice over you" (Isa. 62:4–5).

> *Father, I pray that You give me fresh revelation of You as "Father" in my life. Oh, that I may know Your love in a deeper way. I pray that I would gain more insight into the fact that You, the God of the universe, have adopted me as Your own and You delight in me! Abba, what an astounding thought it is to know that You delight in me. I surely didn't do anything to deserve Your love or Your delight, and yet I am deeply grateful to receive both.*

The Lord Delights in You

You're wondering if God likes you? I tell you—
you are the very object of His affection.

—ALLEN HOOD

HOW WE VIEW God determines how we approach Him in prayer. If we view Him as aloof or angry, we will not want to pray very much. When we see God as a tender Father and Jesus as a loving Bridegroom who desires for us to come to Him in a deep relationship, then we will pray much more.

The Lord is raising up a multitude of men and women—singers, preachers, evangelists, writers, intercessors, people in the workplace—all over the world who will proclaim that God delights in His people. Then it will become normal for God's people to grow confident in His affections for them instead of drawing back in shame as many do today.

Many Christians do not have a picture of God as a person who delights in His people with a heart of gladness. In fact, I believe that many view God as mostly mad or sad. But the truth is that His heart is filled with gladness over us (Zeph. 3:17), and appropriating this powerful truth will help us to grow in prayer with great confidence.

WHAT CAN I DO?

Proclaim the words of Zephaniah 3:17 before you pray. Say out loud that the Father's heart is filled with gladness over you.

FOR REFLECTION

"The LORD your God in your midst, the Mighty One, will save; He will rejoice over you with gladness, He will quiet *you* with His love, He will rejoice over you with singing" (Zeph. 3:17).

Lord, I remind myself that You are not like earthly fathers, all of whom are imperfect. But You are altogether different. Thank You for delighting in me, even when I don't feel delightful. I pray that You would give me more insight into Your heart as my Father, helping me to realize that I am the object of Your affection and delight. I pray today that I may know and experience the wholehearted love with which You love me.

Day 30

Too Busy to Pray?

As if you could kill time without injuring eternity.
—Henry David Thoreau

In Ephesians 5 the apostle Paul challenged the believers in Ephesus to spend their time wisely, telling them in verse 16 to "[redeem] the time, because the days are evil." To redeem our time is to use it with the utmost care so that we may grow in God and extend His kingdom. It involves setting godly and wise priorities for the use of our time.

If we do not schedule our time, others will seize it and we will end up living in the tyranny of the urgent, giving ourselves to whatever opportunity, social event, need, or crisis presents itself to us in the moment. I have known people who lived at the whim of everyone and everything that came their way. But when they looked back over the years, they sadly admitted that many of those pressures, opportunities, and "urgent matters" had not been connected to their destiny in God or the assignment He had given them in life. *Live by what is important, not by the tyranny of the urgent.* Time is a nonrenewable resource in our lives—once we spend it, we can't get it back.

Establishing time for prayer is one way that we can redeem our time—our time can "purchase" eternal things that last forever. We can invest our time in a way that will lead to our hearts being awakened from the death of passivity and to our experiencing the light of God's presence. Then we will be equipped to love God and people in a far more consistent way. A focused use of time is critical for anyone who desires to have a strong prayer life.

WHAT CAN I DO?

Clear the clutter from your life and time wasted on nonessential or non-meaningful things. Commit to "purchasing" eternal things instead. Take a moment and think about your last few days and the things you have done. How many of those things were done in the "tyranny of the urgent"? Set a time to actually sit and write out a schedule based on your obligations in life, as well as your heart, to seek the Lord. Both are equally important!

FOR REFLECTION

"See then that you walk circumspectly, not as fools but as wise, redeeming the time, because the days are evil" (Eph. 5:15–16).

Father, I choose to make the most of my time by meeting with You on a daily basis—to speak with You and listen to Your voice. By doing so, I know I am purchasing eternal things that will last forever.

Day 31

Sacred Aloneness

*Therefore, whether the desire for prayer is on you or
not, get to your closet at the set time; shut yourself
in with God; wait upon Him and seek His face.*

—R. F. HORTON

THE BIBLICAL CALL to "sacred aloneness" allows us to grow in love.
It energizes us to love God and to love people for the long haul.
Being connected to Jesus at the heart level through prayer is the
lifeline that enables us to sustain ministry in healing the sick and
doing works of justice and compassion for decades without burnout.
We can enter into this "sacred aloneness" both in our private prayer
time as well as when we are in public worship services. The key is to
engage with and talk directly to the Lord.

Prayer was never meant to be only about asking God to give us
things. Rather, it is a place of encounter with God where our spirits
are energized as we grow to love Him more. It positions us to love
God and people by receiving God's love as a Father and a Bridegroom.

We can find time for prayer by avoiding the tendency to waste
time with idle talk; too much television, social media, or recreation;
and an excess of networking (to help our ministries or businesses
grow). We have to say no to certain things, even some good things,
to have time to say yes to growing in prayer.

Time for prayer will not suddenly appear in our schedules. We
have to seize it by saying no to some legitimate activities and pleasures. We can say no even to some important things in our lives
because praying is the most important thing—even the best thing.
Read what Jesus told Martha when she wanted her younger sister,

Mary, to stop sitting at Jesus' feet to help her prepare the meal: "But one thing is needed, and Mary has chosen that good part, which will not be taken away from her" (Luke 10:42).

WHAT CAN I DO?

Schedule time for sacred aloneness, whether in a private prayer time or a public worship or prayer gathering. Deliberately build in time for God-moments, even if that means you have to say no to other things. That way, the Lord won't get the leftovers of your time, energy, passion, etc.

FOR REFLECTION

"But one thing is needed, and Mary has chosen that good part, which will not be taken away from her" (Luke 10:42).

> *Lord, help me to say no to time-wasting activities and say yes to more time in prayer. Like Mary, I want to choose "that good part, which will not be taken away."*

Day 32

Getting Organized

*Faith in a prayer-hearing God will
make a prayer-loving Christian.*

· —ANDREW MURRAY

I USE THREE TYPES of prayer and three prayer themes to organize my own prayer time. The three types of prayer are *intercessory prayer, personal petition,* and *devotional prayer.* (We'll look at the three themes in tomorrow's devotional.)

Intercession is prayer for others—people, places, and organizations. God has ordained intercessory prayer as the means of releasing a greater measure of His power and blessing on individuals, families, businesses, ministries, churches, and the various spheres of society. With intercession we pray for the sick, for friends facing difficulties and families in crisis, for revival in the church, for justice, for the salvation of those who don't know the Lord, for social transformation, and so on.

Personal petition is prayer for the release of God's blessing and favor for our personal lives—our families, finances, ministries, relationships, health, and circumstances. This type of prayer includes praying for your own physical health and protection and for your ministry, as well as for financial increase and blessing, favor in relationships, the opening of new doors of opportunity to impact others, and so on.

Devotional prayer focuses on worshipping God and being strengthened by the Holy Spirit to love and obey God more. We ask to experience more grace on our minds and hearts as we develop an intimate relationship with God. This type of prayer includes connecting with God in worship, meditation on the Word (pray-reading it), and fellowshipping with the Holy Spirit (sometimes known as contemplative prayer).

Praying for the sick is one form of intercession that is not optional. Scripture commands us to pray for the sick and oppressed (Matt. 10:8; Mark 16:17; James 5:14–15). Set your heart to pray for someone who is sick every day for the rest of your life. The Lord wants His people to operate in the supernatural ministry of the Holy Spirit as a lifestyle!

WHAT CAN I DO?

Think about these three different types of prayer. Do you see one that is lacking in your life or seems to be weaker than the other two? If so, try to find ways this week to grow in that area. Connect with your church's prayer chain either by phone, bulletin, or social media. Bring each sick or afflicted person before the Lord, and expect the supernatural to take place!

FOR REFLECTION

"Heal the sick, cleanse the lepers, raise the dead, cast out demons. Freely you have received, freely give" (Matt. 10:8).

> *Father, starting today, my goal is to get organized and approach prayer as the high calling it is. I commit to pray for the sick, intercede for others, make petitions, and worship You as I grow in prayer.*

Day 33

Three Prayer Themes to Use

*The word of God is the food by
which prayer is nourished.*

—E. M. Bounds

I USE THREE PRAYER themes, regardless of what type of prayer I am offering to God: release of the *gifts, fruit,* and *wisdom* of the Holy Spirit. Most of the prayers and promises in the Bible fit into one of these three general prayer themes.

Praying for a greater release of the *gifts of the Spirit* involves praying for the release of God's power, including His supernatural favor, provision, and protection in our lives and in the people or places we pray for. Paul told the believers in Corinth that the working of the gifts of the Spirit in our lives is for the "profit of all" (1 Cor. 12:7–10).

Praying for a greater release of the *fruit of the Spirit* refers to asking for God's character to be formed in our lives or the lives of others. We ask that the fullness of the fruit of the Spirit (Gal. 5:22–23) be established in us and in those for whom we pray. One of the primary ways I pray for a person to have more fruit in his character is to ask the Lord to release to him a spirit of conviction and a spirit of wisdom and revelation regarding God's person.

Praying for a greater release of the *wisdom of the Spirit* is asking for an increase of understanding and insight into God's plans, will, and Word for ourselves or for others. We follow Paul's example of praying for spiritual wisdom and understanding for believers so that they walk in a way that agrees with and pleases the Lord (Col. 1:9–10). Praying for spiritual wisdom includes asking the Holy Spirit for dreams and visions that give insight into His will for our lives as well as insight into His strategic plans for a city, nation, business, church, or other organization.

For more than thirty years I have used these three themes as a "grid" to help me focus my prayers for myself and others. I know they will help you, too.

WHAT CAN I DO?

It's easy to ramble in our prayers, but here's a way you can focus: use these three themes and pray for the release of the gifts, fruit, and wisdom of the Holy Spirit—in your own life, in the lives of others, and in your local church.

FOR REFLECTION

"That...the Father of glory, may give to you the spirit of wisdom and revelation in the knowledge of Him...that you may know...what *is* the exceeding greatness of His power toward us who believe" (Eph. 1:17–19).

> *Lord, I ask for a greater release of the revelation of Jesus and for a greater measure of the gifts of the Spirit, the fruit of the Spirit, and the wisdom of the Spirit in my life.*

Praying Biblical Prayers

*When prayer has become secondary, or incidental,
it has lost its power. Men of prayer are those
who use prayer as they use food, or air.*

—M. E. ANDROSS

A s I MENTIONED earlier, we will pray more often and with greater focus if we develop prayer lists and bring them to our prayer times. When I pray, I usually use prayers that are found in the Bible. The prayers of Jesus, Paul, Peter, and others are recorded for our benefit. I refer to them as the apostolic prayers because they are prayers Jesus and the apostles prayed. Because God never changes, we know these prayers are in God's will.

Below is a look into my own prayer journal. I provided only brief "samples" of my prayers so you can get a sense of what a more developed and complete prayer list may look like. As you read the prayer list below, understand that you can pray all the sample prayers for each person on your list.

(For my wife, Diane, our two sons, and their wives and children):

> Fruit: Father, release the spirit of conviction to them in a
> greater measure (John 16:8) and pour out Your love into
> their hearts by the power of the Spirit (Rom. 5:5). Fill
> them with love for Jesus and for others and with the spirit
> of the fear of the Lord (Phil. 1:9)....
>
> Wisdom: Father, grant my sons wisdom to know Your
> specific will for each area of their lives—their ministries,
> finances, relationships, business ventures, marriages, and
> in raising their children (Col. 1:9–11). Fill Diane with

understanding of Your will for her ministry and business and as a grandmother (Col. 4:12)....

Gifts: Father, give prophetic dreams and visions to Diane, my sons, their wives, and their children (Acts 2:17). Release the spirit of glory and the power of God in their lives and through their words. Grant them favor in relationships and protect them from the attack of the enemy and from all sickness and financial attacks....

I encourage you to write out your prayer list, either in a notebook or on your tablet or laptop, and use it during your prayer times.

WHAT CAN I DO?

Mention each of your family members by name, and ask the Lord to impart the gifts, fruits, and wisdom of the Holy Spirit to each one. Check back in your prayer journal a few months from now to see how their lives have changed.

FOR REFLECTION

"We...do not cease to pray for you, and to ask that you may be filled with the knowledge of His will in all wisdom and spiritual understanding; that you may walk worthy of the Lord, fully pleasing Him" (Col. 1:9–10).

> *Lord, I come before You using the very prayers that moved Your heart in the days of old when You first gave them to the apostles by the Holy Spirit.*

Five Steps to Effective Prayer

(STEPS 1–3)

> *Before a word of petition is offered, we should*
> *have the definite and vivid consciousness that*
> *we are talking to God, and should believe that*
> *He is listening to our petition and is going*
> *to grant the thing that we ask of Him.*
>
> —R. A. TORREY

NOW THAT WE know what prayer is, why we pray, and how to ensure that our prayers will be effective, let's consider the five "steps" we are to take when we actually *pray*. Taking these steps will ensure that we are following a biblical paradigm or perspective for prayer.

Though there is no place in Scripture that provides us with a one-two-three formula of how to pray, I believe that as we study the whole teaching of Scripture, we find that these five steps are part of the process. They will help us to grow in prayer and to understand how perseverance relates to receiving answers to our prayers.

Step 1: Verbalize your requests to God. Many times people think about all the things they need or want but never actually *pray* about them. For such people, the words of the apostle James are apt: "You do not have because you do not ask" (James 4:2).

Step 2: Receive your requests in the spirit realm. When we pray according to God's will, we know that He hears and approves of the request, thus we can believe with confidence that we have *received it in the spirit realm.* We receive our prayers in two ways. First we receive them in the spirit realm, and later we have them in the natural, when we see them with our eyes. However, before we receive them in the spirit, God must hear and approve of our prayers. Remember, many circumstantial prayer requests are not promised in Scripture, so sometimes we cannot be sure that the Lord has approved our request until He answers it.

Step 3: Believe that you receive what you ask for. Jesus spoke of the necessity of first believing that we receive the things we ask for (in the spirit realm) as the condition for receiving them in the natural, earthly realm. When we ask something in God's will, we must believe that we have the "title deed" to our answer (we receive it in the spirit realm) and that in due time the answer will be manifest in the natural realm.

We will look at Steps 4 and 5 tomorrow.

WHAT CAN I DO?

As you pray today, visualize yourself owning the "title deed" to your answers in the spirit realm. Believe that in due time you will see the answers manifest in the natural realm.

FOR REFLECTION

"Therefore, I say to you, whatever things you ask when you pray, believe that you receive them [in the spirit], and you will have them [in the natural]" (Mark 11:24).

> *Lord, thank You that every prayer that agrees with Your Word and heart is a prayer whose answer I have already received from You in the spirit realm.*

Five Steps to Effective Prayer

(STEPS 4–5)

Prayer is weakness leaning on omnipotence.
—W. S. BOWD

WE MUST BE aware of the distinction between the spiritual and the natural realms to understand how prayer works. How do our requests move from the spiritual realm to the natural realm? Through holy, persevering, believing prayer.

Step 4: Remind God of His Word. This fourth step is essential. We are to consistently remind the Lord of what He promised us and of what He has already given us in the spirit realm, as the prophet Isaiah makes clear: "You who remind the LORD, take no rest for yourselves; and give Him no rest until He establishes [what He promised]" (Isa. 62:6–7, NASB).

In prayer we state our cause and put God in remembrance of His Word and what He has already given us in the spirit realm in Christ or of what He has promised to give us related to our personal circumstances. (See Isaiah 43:26.) We remind God of His promises and thank Him for having already given them to us in the spirit and for the certainty of their being manifested in the natural in God's timing. As we continually remind God of His promises with thanksgiving, we position ourselves to receive them in the natural realm.

Step 5: Receive your requests in the natural realm. Prayers that are in God's will are always answered in God's timing and in God's way, so do not give up too quickly or become discouraged if the answer to your prayer is delayed. There are reasons God delays answers, as we will see. Again, we must receive every request *twice*—first in the spirit, and then eventually in the natural. God does not always give His answer as one big downpour of blessing. Sometimes the answer comes in stages over months, years, or even decades.

We can trust His amazing leadership in the timing and method in which He answers our prayers. It is not our responsibility to fix the timing or the circumstances of our expected blessing; we are simply to be faithful and patient in prayer.

WHAT CAN I DO?

Remind God of His Word, especially as time passes and you don't see your answer on the horizon. Hold fast. Proclaim His promises back to Him, receive your answers in the spirit realm, and wait patiently. Your answer will come!

FOR REFLECTION

"Put Me in remembrance; let us contend together; state your case" (Isa. 43:26).

> *Lord, I remind You of Your promises to me today and receive each one, first in the spirit and eventually in the natural according to Your perfect timing.*

_____

_____

_____

_____

_____

_____

_____

_____

Day 37

Why Does God Delay Answers?

*Whole days or weeks have I spent prostrate
on the ground in silent or vocal prayer.*

—GEORGE WHITEFIELD

ONE OF THE most common questions Christians ask about prayer
is why God delays answers to prayers, especially when they seem
to be clearly in accordance with His will. Several factors may con-
tribute to a delay, including God's timing, demonic resistance, man's
free will, the Lord's desire for partnership with His people, and the
value He places on our being in unity with His heart and with one
another. Let's very briefly consider a few of these factors:

+ God's timing is often very different from ours.

+ Demonic resistance can cause a delay in our
  receiving an answer to prayer. The resistance is
  removed as we persistently wrestle against demonic
  powers (Eph. 6:12; Dan. 10:13).

+ Man can use his free will to do evil, and God
  may allow it for a season. Thus the answer to our
  prayers is seemingly delayed, but only until the Lord
  removes the hindrances caused by evil actions.

+ The Lord desires partnership with His people, so
  He encourages us to persevere in prayer.

+ Sometimes God waits to release the answer to a
  prayer until His people are in unity with Him in

righteousness and in unity with one another in
humility and love.

The exact combination of these factors is somewhat mysterious, so we must trust Jesus' wise and loving leadership regarding the reason prayers that are according to God's will are delayed or seemingly not answered at all.

WHAT CAN I DO?

Remember that God's ways are higher than your ways. Sometimes an answer is delayed because the Lord wants to bring something better along in His perfect timing.

FOR REFLECTION

"But the prince of the kingdom of Persia withstood me twenty-one days; and behold, Michael, one of the chief princes, came to help me, for I had been left alone there with the kings of Persia" (Dan. 10:13).

Lord, when I remember that Your timing in answering my prayers is often different from mine—yet always right on time—I remain in peace because I trust Your leadership.

Day 38

You're in Good Company

Our prayers lay the track down [on] which God's power can come. Like a mighty locomotive, its power is irresistible, but it cannot reach us without rails.

—WATCHMAN NEE

WE ARE NOT always sure about what God has promised to fully release in this age related to our circumstances—what He will partially and progressively release now and what He will fully release in the age to come. However, we can be sure of this: God is loving and faithful, His Word is true, and He answers prayer. Therefore, we must guard against giving up and falling into unbelief when our prayers are not answered in the time frame that we would choose.

Examples of delayed answers to prayer abound in the lives of all believers, including heroes of the faith such as E. M. Bounds, Hudson Taylor, Andrew Murray, William Carey, and Charles Spurgeon. One great man of God, George Müller, prayed daily for fifty-two years for a loved one to be saved. The answer to his prayer came shortly after Müller died.[1]

Our prayer requests move from the spiritual realm to the natural realm through holy, persevering, believing prayer. Many people give up too quickly. They offer their prayers a few times and then lose heart, moving on to other things rather than persevering. Persevering prayer is continually reminding God of what He has already given us and what He promises to yet give us, and continually asking Him to manifest the full measure of each blessing in the natural.

If we understand the distinction between receiving our requests in the spiritual and the natural realms, then we will see the value of persevering prayer. Knowing how prayer works will give us the courage to rise up and ask and keep on asking until we receive all that the Lord has for us.

WHAT CAN I DO?

Don't give up on your prayers. Show God that you have "stick-to-it-iveness" by persevering in prayer, reminding Him of His promises, and then waiting with active faith—the kind of faith that lives "as if."

FOR REFLECTION

"Be joyful in hope, patient in affliction, faithful in prayer" (Rom. 12:12, NIV).

> *Lord, sometimes I get frustrated when I don't see an answer to my prayers, but I know You are faithful and Your ways are higher than my ways. Help me to persevere in prayer! Lord, I pray that You would help me to see the big picture and that You are faithful. Teach my heart to trust in Your leadership and to not lose heart over the amount of time that passes before I see the answer to my prayers.*

Day 39

The Spoken Word Releases Power

*We must begin to believe that God, in the
mystery of prayer, has entrusted us with a
force that can move the heavenly world, and
can bring its power down to earth.*

—ANDREW MURRAY

IT WOULD BE impossible for me to overemphasize the importance of intercessory prayer. Why? Because God has chosen intercession as the primary means of releasing His power in the earth. Scripture makes it clear that intercession is one of the central activities in God's kingdom, both now and in the age to come.

The fact that Jesus, the divine Son of God, intercedes reveals how important intercession is. Jesus is fully God and fully Man, the second person of the Trinity, and yet He intercedes and releases the Father's power. He will still be making intercession a million years from now.

We see Jesus' work in the phrase "and God said" ten times in Genesis 1 (KJV). The foundational principle of intercession is that the Father's plans were spoken by Jesus, and then the Holy Spirit released power. David wrote that "by the word of the LORD the heavens were made" (Ps. 33:6). The apostle John confirmed Jesus' role in creation when he wrote, "All things were made through Him [Jesus], and without Him nothing was made that was made" (John 1:3).

The Father has ordained that His ideas must be spoken, and when they are spoken, the Spirit releases power. A foundational law of the kingdom is that the Spirit moves in response to God's Word being spoken by His people. Whether Jesus is speaking over the formless heavens and the earth at creation or we are interceding for revival at a prayer meeting, God's power is released through the principle of intercession, speaking God's Word back to God.

WHAT CAN I DO?

Take intercession seriously and speak God's Word back to Him, declaring that His kingdom come in situations and people on earth as it is (already) in heaven.

FOR REFLECTION

"God...has in these last days spoken to us by His Son...through whom also He made the worlds; who being the brightness of His glory and the express image of His person, and upholding all things by the word of His power..." (Heb. 1:1–3).

> *Lord, because You have chosen intercession as the primary means of releasing Your power in the earth, I thank You for the honor and privilege to partner with You in intercession.*

Day 40

His Words in Our Mouth

*[Prayer] can be best performed after the inner
man has been nourished by meditation on
the Word of God. Through His Word, our
Father speaks to us, encourages us, comforts
us, instructs us, humbles us, and reproves us.*

—GEORGE MÜLLER

A S PART OF our spiritual armor, we have the sword of the Spirit, which is God's Word. It is a powerful weapon when spoken and released against darkness. In Paul's encouragement to the Ephesians to be strong in God and in the power of His might, he wrote, "Put on the whole armor of God, that you may be able to stand against the wiles of the devil.... Take... the sword of the Spirit, which is the Word of God; praying always" (Eph. 6:11, 17–18).

When tempted by Satan, Jesus spoke the Word of God, which went forth like a sword striking Satan's domain (Matt. 4:3–7). As we speak God's Word, we can release strength to a friend's heart. We call it "encouragement" because it gives him courage, or strength. Our prayer is God's way of releasing His power so that the friend can overcome condemnation or discouragement or other trials in his life. One way we grow in prayer is by speaking God's Word against Satan's lies that assault our hearts.

Much can be achieved in the Lord's purposes when we declare His Word. The Lord put His words in the mouth of the prophet Jeremiah to bring about His desired changes in the nations (Jer. 1:9–10). The Lord has ordained that for all eternity He will put His words into our mouths so that we are able to intercede and release His power on the earth.

WHAT CAN I DO?

Recite the "whole armor of God" passage from Ephesians 6 often, and as you speak about each piece of armor think of it as "dressing" yourself. Take that armor seriously, and use it in your prayers for yourself and others.

FOR REFLECTION

"I have put My words in your mouth. See, I have this day set you over the nations and over the kingdoms, to root out and to pull down...to build and to plant" (Jer. 1:9–10).

Father, by the grace of God, I am determined to put Your words in my mouth and to say what You say about the circumstances around me. What a privilege it is to partner with You in establishing Your kingdom on earth.

Day 41

Intercession Deepens Our Intimacy With God

Those persons who know the deep peace
of God that passes all understanding, are
always men and women of much prayer.

—R. A. TORREY

NTERCESSION HAS MANY benefits beyond a greater release of God's power to others. Over the next several days we will look at the key benefits it bestows on the intercessor. Intercession draws us into intimacy, transforms our hearts, unifies us in community, renews our faith, multiplies blessing back on us, and gives us an inheritance in the people and places we pray for. Let's look at the first benefit: intercession deepens intimacy and leads to transformation.

Intercession helps us to grow in intimacy with God and transforms our hearts by causing us to internalize God's Word as we pray it back to Him. Because Jesus' words are spirit and life (John 6:63), they have the power to impart life to us as we speak them. Each time we say what God says, it "marks" our hearts and changes us in a small measure because we receive a small impartation of His life. This progressively renews our minds and tenderizes our hearts.

Think of a computer programmer who writes many lines of code while developing a computer program. Spiritually, we are doing something comparable to this. We "write a line of code" on our hearts every time we speak God's Word back to Him in prayer. It marks our hearts even though we cannot accurately measure the change in weeks or months. Over the years the change inside us is profound.

Our prayers for others affect our own hearts more than we know. We may not feel anything when praying for a nation that is remote and far away. However, there is an accumulated impact on our lives that often goes unnoticed.

I encourage those who are beginners in prayer or who have not been consistent in prayer to start today—take small steps on your journey to grow in prayer and watch what God will do in your life.

WHAT CAN I DO?

Write new lines of code on your heart today by speaking God's Word back to Him. As you do, notice how your faith rises up and a holy boldness infuses your spirit.

FOR REFLECTION

"The words that I [Jesus] speak to you are spirit, and they are life" (John 6:63).

> *Lord, I'm ready and willing to take small steps on my journey of growing in prayer. As I step out in faith, I trust that You hear me and remember my prayers—and touch my heart in the process!*

_____

_____

_____

_____

_____

_____

_____

_____

Day 42

Intercession Increases Understanding

*There is no other activity in life so important
as that of prayer. Every other activity depends
upon prayer for its best efficiency.*

—M. E. Andross

Intercession releases spiritual insight (Eph. 1:17). As Daniel prayed with persistence, Gabriel visited him and gave him "skill to understand" spiritual things:

> Now while I was speaking, praying...and presenting my supplication before the LORD...yes, while I was speaking in prayer, the man Gabriel...said, "O Daniel, I have now come forth to give you skill to understand. At the beginning of your supplications the command went out, and I have come to tell you, for you are greatly beloved...understand the vision."
>
> —Daniel 9:20–23

Paul prayed that the saints would grow in understanding:

> That the God of our Lord Jesus Christ, the Father of glory, may give to you the spirit of wisdom and revelation in the knowledge of Him, the eyes of your understanding being enlightened; that you may know...
>
> —Ephesians 1:17–18

As we spend time in the Father's presence, not only are we transformed, but we grow in wisdom and understanding of spiritual things. I don't know about you, but for me that is a worthy quest—one that promises not only to fulfill the longings of our heart but to transform us into the image of Christ.

WHAT CAN I DO?

Ask the Father to increase your spiritual understanding of His heart and discernment of His will and ways. As you practice using this "muscle," you'll notice that your discernment of spiritual things grows sharper.

FOR REFLECTION

"And this I pray, that your love may abound still more and more in knowledge and all discernment" (Phil. 1:9).

> *Lord, reveal Your love for me and impart in me love for You more and more. I pray that You will change my heart so that I love You in a deeper way. Give me more insight that I may better understand spiritual things. I want to be transformed by Your indwelling Spirit.*

_____

_____

_____

_____

_____

_____

_____

_____

_____

_____

Day 43

Intercession Unites Us in Community

*A man who is intimate with God will
never be intimidated by men.*

—Leonard Ravenhill

NTERCESSION RELEASES GOD'S power and justice as it changes the spiritual atmosphere of cities (Luke 18:8). Intercession also unites our hearts to the people and places we pray for. We will grow to love who and what we pray for. In addition, we will love those we consistently pray *with*. It is impossible to pray for, or with, anyone regularly without eventually feeling love for that person. As John Calvin wrote, "To make intercession for men is the most powerful and practical way in which we can express our love for them."[1] Intercession unifies people, and it is a practical expression of loving people as it releases deliverance for the needy and unites our heart to the people and places for which we pray.

Another profound benefit of intercession is that it renews our faith as we speak God's Word back to Him in prayer. Praying biblical prayers builds our faith for revival. The very act of praying the Word results in strengthening our faith for the promises we pray for. You will find that your faith grows stronger and stronger as you develop the practice of speaking the Word back to the Father in intercession.

WHAT CAN I DO?

Ask the leadership of your church if they will schedule a time when the whole body can come together for a corporate prayer time—an

87

intercessory prayer meeting where you target and lift up the community where God has set you! If that's not possible, invite two or three praying friends to join you for a day and night of "watchman on the wall" (see Isaiah 62:6) intercessory prayer.

FOR REFLECTION

"This will turn out for my deliverance through your prayer" (Phil. 1:19).

> *Lord, as I speak Your Word back to You, I rejoice to see my faith renewed, my love for others grow stronger, and my prayers answered. I take joy in partnering with Your heart to see revival in my city.*

Day 44

Intercession Multiplies Blessings

*Praying men are the vice-regents of God; they
do His work and carry out His plans.*

—E. M. BOUNDS

INTERCESSION FOR OTHERS causes multiplied blessings to return back on the life and family of the intercessor. Every prayer of blessing for another is a prayer that God returns back on you and your loved ones. Jesus promised: "Give, and it will be given to you: good measure, pressed down...will be put into your bosom. For with the same measure that you use, it will be measured back to you" (Luke 6:38).

The law of the kingdom requires that we always receive more than we give away. The measure that we give in prayer for others will be measured back to us. This is one of my favorite promises about prayer. It does not matter for whom we pray. Even when we pray for our enemies as Jesus commands us to do, we end up being blessed by the prayers we pray on their behalf.

When we pray for our enemies, we are forced to deal with our own bad attitudes and to get our spirits right. But we also become the recipients of our prayers. For example, when we pray for the release of the spirit of wisdom on our enemies, we receive wisdom as well.

The principle of multiplied blessings applies to all we do in God's will, whether we are offering prayer, giving money or mercy, or serving people in small ways. The Lord multiplies blessing back to us in a hundredfold way. We will never, ever "out-give" God. Every

Spirit-inspired prayer we pray will be "turned back" on us and our loved ones.

WHAT CAN I DO?

Set your heart to give with a spirit of joyful abandon, trusting that you can never out-give God. Find someone in special need and give them an anonymous gift.

FOR REFLECTION

"There is no one who has left house or brothers or sisters or father or mother or wife or children or lands, for My sake and the gospel's, who shall not receive a hundredfold now in this time...and in the age to come, eternal life" (Mark 10:29–30).

> *Lord, thank You for Your remarkable generosity and atten-tiveness to multiply everything that is given to You in love. It is so glorious that we can never out-give You! Lord, thank You that Your eyes are on me and that nothing goes unseen. I pray for faith and an expectancy to see a return on the things that I have sown in secret!*

Day 45

Intercession Gives Us
an Inheritance

*If we want to see mighty wonders wrought
in the place of weakness and failure, let us
answer God's challenge, "Call unto me, and
I will answer thee, and show thee great and
mighty things which thou knowest not!"*

—HUDSON TAYLOR

INTERCESSION GIVES US an "inheritance" in the people and places
we pray for. We have a spiritual investment with a sense of owner-
ship, as well as eternal blessing and joy in all the people and places
that we regularly pray for and serve.

> For what is our hope, or joy, or crown of rejoicing? Is it not
> even you in the presence of our Lord Jesus Christ at His
> coming? For you are our glory and joy.
>
> —1 THESSALONIANS 2:19–20

This inheritance begins in this age and continues in the age to
come. When we pray for Egypt, Japan, Iran, or another nation, our
prayers release blessing on that nation. They release blessing on us
and our families as well, and we receive an inheritance in what happens in that country, in this age and in the age to come.

Our inheritance in intercession has a long-term impact. Our
prayers for people and cities have an impact both now and in the
age to come. The prayers of the saints from history are stored in a
bowl near God's throne and have an impact in the end times (Rev.
5:8; 8:1–6).

WHAT CAN I DO?

Here's another exercise for your prayer journal: write down the "inheritance" you have in the people and situations you pray for. Check back periodically (because time passes so fast) to see how the Lord has answered and blessed you related to the prayers you have prayed. They are a true investment into others.

·FOR REFLECTION

"Ask of Me [in prayer], and I will give You the nations for Your inheritance" (Ps. 2:8).

> *Father, I lay claim to the inheritance I have in the people and places I pray for. What a wonderful God You are—You allow me to partner with You in bringing about the fulfillment of Your purposes on earth. I thank You for giving me Your heart for different nations. I pray that as I journey in this season, You will begin to open my heart even more to pray for them more strategically. I thank You that You have so much in Your heart for them and that You are sharing that with me as I lift them up in prayer.*

Day 46

Apostolic Prayers From the Bible

Prayer does not change the purpose of God.
But prayer does change the action of God.

—CHUCK SMITH

WHEN I INTERCEDE, I almost always use the prayers in the Bible. The prayers that Jesus, Paul, and Peter prayed are recorded for our benefit. I refer to them as the "apostolic prayers" because they are the prayers that Jesus prayed as our chief apostle (Heb. 3:1) and that the Holy Spirit gave to the apostles who were His followers. Below are some examples:

- Acts 4:24–31 (A prayer for impartation of Holy Spirit boldness along with an increase of signs and wonders)

- Romans 15:5–7 (A prayer for unity in the church across a city)

- Romans 15:13 (A prayer to be filled with supernatural joy, peace, and hope)

- Romans 10:1 (A prayer for Israel to be saved through Jesus)

- 1 Corinthians 1:4–8 (A prayer to be enriched with the supernatural gifts of the Holy Spirit, leading to righteousness)

- Ephesians 1:17–19 (A prayer to receive the revelation of Jesus' beauty, to see how greatly He values His people as His inheritance, and to walk in a greater measure of the power of God)

+ Ephesians 3:16–19 (A prayer for the supernatural strengthening of the heart and a deeper experience of God's love)

+ Philippians 1:9–11 (A prayer for God's love to abound in our hearts, resulting in discernment and a deep commitment to righteousness)

+ Colossians 1:9–12 (A prayer to know God's will, to be fruitful in ministry, and to be strengthened by intimacy with God as we do the work of the kingdom)

+ 1 Thessalonians 3:9–13 (A prayer for the release of effective ministry to strengthen believers so they will abound in love and holiness)

+ 2 Thessalonians 1:11–12 (A prayer to be equipped and prepared to walk in the fullness of God's destiny for the church and its people)

+ 2 Thessalonians 3:1–5 (A prayer for the Word to increase by the release of Holy Spirit power and to encounter the love of God in a greater way)

In 1979, when I first began to lead daily prayer meetings, I used the apostolic prayers simply because I didn't know what else to do. It was one of those real-life encounters when God grabbed hold of my life and apprehended me and said, "You are an intercessor." I got up in front of my church of young adults and said, "I am an intercessor." They said, "What's that?" I said, "I don't have a clue." I truly had no idea what an intercessor was! I went to the bookstores in town and bought books on intercession. There were hardly any.

I was so clueless at first about what to do in a prayer meeting that I didn't even know what we would pray, so I wrote out by hand the apostolic prayers. I have since learned that the apostolic prayers in the Bible are a valuable gift to the church: they are the prayers that burned in God's heart for His people. They give us the language of His heart, and because God never changes, we can be assured that they are still burning in His heart. These prayers are guaranteed! They are like checks already signed in heaven and waiting only for a cosigner on the earth before they are cashed. And they are as relevant today as they were in the early church.

WHAT CAN I DO?

Take three apostolic prayers today and pray them out loud in your private prayer time. Keep the words of those prayers alive in your spirit as you go about your day. The Lord hears you.

FOR REFLECTION

"Therefore we also pray always for you that our God would count you worthy of this calling, and fulfill all the good pleasure of His goodness and the work of faith with power" (2 Thess. 1:11).

> *Lord, just as the apostolic prayers burn in Your heart, so make them burn in my heart. I want to be considered by You as a faithful prayer warrior for Your kingdom.*

Day 47

Apostolic Prayers Are God-Centered and Positive

*Prayer strikes the winning blow; service
is simply picking up the pieces.*

—S. D. GORDON

ALL THE PRAYERS in the New Testament are God-centered prayers: each one is addressed to God. *Not one apostolic prayer is addressed to the devil.* God-centered prayer, including spiritual warfare prayer, is the model set forth in the New Testament. It is the model the early church used in resisting and dislodging demonic spiritual forces and cultural strongholds (Eph. 6:12; 2 Cor. 10:3–5).

All the prayers of Jesus that are recorded in the Scripture were directed to the Father (John 14:16; 17:5, 11, 15, 25). Jesus taught His disciples to direct their prayers to the Father as well (Matt. 18:19; Luke 11:2, 13). The apostles' prayers followed Jesus' example, and they also teach us to address the Father when we pray. In the great "warfare epistle" Paul wrote to the Ephesians, he addressed all his prayers to the Father (Eph. 1:16–17; 3:14, 16, 20).

The apostolic prayers are also "positive" prayers: they ask God to release good qualities rather than asking Him to remove negative qualities. For example, the apostle Paul prayed for love to abound rather than asking the Lord to remove hatred (Phil. 1:9). He prayed for unity instead of praying against division (Rom. 15:5–7). He asked for an increase of the spirit of peace rather than the removal of the spirit of fear (Rom. 15:13). He did not pray against sin but asked for an increase of holiness, purity, and love (1 Thess. 3:12–13). Even

Paul's requests to be delivered from evil men focus on the deliverance of God's people rather than on exposing or bringing down the evil men who were persecuting him (2 Thess. 3:2–3).

The Father knew that praying for the impartation of positive virtues instead of focusing on removing negative characteristics would *unify* intercessors and *heal* some of the negative emotions against the church in the person who is praying. Our emotions are impacted in a positive, loving way as we come before our loving Father day after day to pray for His goodness to increase in the church.

WHAT CAN I DO?

Start to phrase your prayers in a positive way. Instead of praying against evil or speaking to the devil, direct your prayers to the Father and ask for the increase of holiness, purity, and love.

FOR REFLECTION

"For this reason I bow my knees to the Father of our Lord Jesus Christ...that He would grant you, according to the riches of His glory, to be strengthened with might through His Spirit in the inner man" (Eph. 3:14–16).

Father, I agree with Your Word when I pray and ask for the impartation of positive virtues of the kingdom instead of focusing on what is wrong in my life or circumstances. Thy kingdom come!

_____

_____

_____

_____

_____

Day 48

Healed by the Great Psychologist

*Prayer "is the root, the fountain, the
mother of a thousand blessings."*

—CHRYSOSTOM

INOTICED CHANGE IN my own life in the early days as I regularly
prayed the apostolic prayers for the church with their positive language. Little by little I became more positive in my emotions and
developed more mercy and kindness in my heart toward the weaknesses in the church.

The positive focus of the apostolic prayers is also essential in
helping us to operate in faith. The apostolic prayers in the New
Testament provide us with good theology for a victorious church.
Praying these prayers builds our faith for revival.

A man once asked me, "Why do you believe the church will be
victorious at the end of the age?" I told him to look at the prayers
of Jesus and the apostles for the church. My theology on a victorious church and revival was formed partially by praying the New
Testament prayers repeatedly. These prayers were given by the Holy
Spirit, and though they have not yet been fully answered, they surely
will be. The church will walk in great victory, power, purity, unity,
and love before Jesus returns.

Positive prayers facilitate unity; impact our emotions, and build
our faith. The Father is the "Great Psychologist." He designed these
prayers to help human hearts flow right and work together in unity
with a spirit of encouragement.

WHAT CAN I DO?

Notice how your moods and emotions change as you begin to utter positive prayers. Allow the Great Psychologist to renew your mind, literally, as you proclaim His goodness from a thankful heart. There's healing in virtue.

FOR REFLECTION

"And this I pray, that your love may abound still more and more in knowledge and all discernment" (Phil. 1:9).

> *Lord, as I focus on and agree with Your heart and promises, my faith is stirred, mercy and kindness grow in my heart, and I have the boldness to proclaim those things that align with Your will.*

_____

_____

_____

_____

_____

_____

_____

_____

_____

_____

_____

_____

_____

Day 49

A Strong Church
Transforms Culture

*I fear the prayers of John Knox more than
all the assembled armies of Europe.*

—MARY QUEEN OF SCOTS

IT IS IMPORTANT to note that the vast majority of the apostolic prayers
are focused on strengthening the church, not on the lost or the transformation of society. This does not mean that God is ambivalent about
the lost or society or that we are not to pray for these things. However,
the only prayer in the New Testament that is specifically focused on the
lost is found in Romans 10:1, where Paul entreats, "Brethren, my heart's
desire and prayer to God for Israel is that they may be saved."

Why the overwhelming focus on strengthening and reviving the
church? Because God's primary strategy and plan to reach the lost
or to impact a city is by anointing His church with power, love, and
wisdom. When we pray for the whole church in a particular city to
be revived in love and power, the answer to these prayers will have an
immense impact on the lost in that city. Many unbelievers will inevitably come to Jesus, and society will be changed as the church walks
in the power of the Holy Spirit.

We see this principle at work in the city of Ephesus. What was
the result of the prayers for the church in this city? The preaching of
the Word of God was so powerfully anointed that its influence "grew
mightily and prevailed" across the entire city (Acts 19:20). God's
strategy was to raise up a large anointed church there that would
win a great harvest all across Asia. What happened in Ephesus was

so powerful that everyone who lived in Asia "heard the word of the Lord" from Paul and others in this church.

When preachers are anointed and the church is revived, the saints will speak the Word and do the works of the kingdom with great consistency, and a multitude of unbelievers will come to Jesus. Therefore, we do well to labor in prayer for an increased anointing of the Spirit on the church, knowing that a harvest will surely result. No power can prevent the lost from coming to Jesus in great numbers when the church is revived and operating together in the anointing of the Spirit.

WHAT CAN I DO?

Keep praying for an increased anointing on the proclamation of the Word, that it will go forth with boldness that will convict unbelievers of their need for a Savior (John 16:8). If altar calls are given at your church, intercede silently at the moment of decision, asking the Father to draw them by His Spirit. And read books on revival and see what God did when people came together and cried out for revival in their generation.

FOR REFLECTION

"And many who had believed [in Ephesus] came confessing and telling their deeds...So the word of the Lord grew mightily and prevailed" (Acts 19:18–20).

> *Lord, I ask that You anoint the preaching of the Word in my city and revive Your church so that we may do the works of the kingdom with boldness and see mighty demonstrations of Your power!*

Day 50

Loving the Lost, Loving Our Enemies

To make intercession for men is the most powerful and practical way in which we can express our love for them.

—JOHN CALVIN

A S I MENTIONED before, we will love those whom we pray for consistently. One reason God requires us to bless and pray for our enemies is because in doing so, we begin to love them. And that is what He is looking for—a heart of love, compassion, and forgiveness, even for those who offend us. If we pray for our enemies, our hearts will eventually become tender toward them. In other words, it is impossible to pray for anyone regularly without eventually loving him.

God knows that we will love the church more as we pray for it regularly. God wants the hearts of the intercessors to connect with the church in the city for which they consistently pray. This is His divine strategy of love.

It is easier to love the lost in a different city or nation because we do not know most of them. But some are quick to become frustrated and impatient with the churches in their own cities because they actually know the believers. Therefore the Lord calls us to pray for the church so that we will love it while we are working to bring the lost to Jesus and impact society. He doesn't want us to despise the church in our city because of the weaknesses we see in the people in various congregations or the way their leaders do things; He wants us to love both the church and the lost.

God is a brilliant strategist! He directs us to pray for the harvest by asking Him to visit the whole church—the local churches—in our area with His great power. It is no coincidence that most of the New Testament prayers are for the church!

WHAT CAN I DO?

Ask the Father to work His brilliant strategy in the harvest field you're praying for and to make you a vibrant part of that harvest time.

FOR REFLECTION

"But I say to you, love your enemies, bless those who curse you, do good to those who hate you, and pray for those who spitefully use you and persecute you, that you may be sons of your Father in heaven" (Matt. 5:44–45).

> *Lord, tenderize my heart as I pray for my enemies. Bless those who mock me, those who offend me, and those who curse me. Give me the compassion of Jesus as I lift them before Your throne.*

_____

_____

_____

_____

_____

_____

_____

_____

Day 51

Using the Apostolic Prayers

*Prayer wonderfully clears the vision; steadies
the nerves; defines duty; stiffens the purpose;
sweetens and strengthens the spirit.*

—S. D. Gordon

As A RULE our prayers should be God-centered prayers, rather
than demon-centered or sin-focused prayers. This is the New
Testament model of prayer, set forth especially by Paul. Below are
suggested ways to pray for the church using the apostolic prayers.

+ Pray for the presence of God to be powerfully manifested in church services and for people to be saved,
  set free, healed, and refreshed by the Spirit during
  the worship, preaching, and ministry times.

+ Pray that love will abound and that believers will
  approve the things that God calls excellent (Phil.
  1:9–10).

+ Pray that the anointing of conviction will rest on
  the preaching of the Word so that both believers
  and unbelievers are impacted greatly (John 16:8).
  Pray for a spirit of holiness and love to prevail in the
  congregation.

+ Pray for a great increase of the gifts of the Spirit
  in the church and the manifestation of these gifts
  through words of knowledge, words of wisdom, dis-
  cerning of spirits, healings, miracles, and so on.

- Pray for a prophetic spirit to rest on preachers, worship teams, and ministry leaders, according to Acts 2:17.

- Pray that the Spirit will open more doors to minister to unbelievers and that He will prepare them to receive the gospel (Col. 4:3; 2 Thess. 3:1).

- Pray that the Spirit will motivate more believers to share the gospel and give more believers a burden for evangelism (Matt. 9:37–38).

- Pray for the spirit of wisdom and revelation in the knowledge of God, His will, and His ways to be given to leaders of churches and the individual members (Eph. 1:17).

- Pray that believers will be strengthened with might by the Spirit in their inner man (Eph. 3:16).

- Pray for unity among all the believers and all the families in the church (John 17:21–23).

- Pray for an increase of the spirit of prayer to be released in the church (Zech. 12:10).

- Pray for every family member to be saved and healed, and for every family to prosper with secure, steady jobs (3 John 2).

If we pray consistently and faithfully in this manner for the church in our cities, over time we will see both the church and the cities transformed before our eyes.

WHAT CAN I DO?

Focus on one of the above prayers each day for the next twelve days.

FOR REFLECTION

"And when He has come, He will convict the world of sin, and of righteousness, and of judgment" (John 16:8).

> *Father, I ask that Your presence be powerfully manifested in church services across this nation and for people to be saved, set free, healed, and refreshed by the Spirit.*

Day 52

Our Most Famous Apostolic Prayer

Prayer is the acid test of devotion.

—SAMUEL CHADWICK

THE MOST FAMOUS, or well-known, apostolic prayer in history is probably the Lord's Prayer as recorded in Matthew's Gospel:

> Our Father in heaven, hallowed be Your name. Your kingdom come. Your will be done on earth as it is in heaven. Give us this day our daily bread. And forgive us our debts, as we forgive our debtors. And do not lead us into temptation, but deliver us from the evil one. For Yours is the kingdom and the power and the glory forever. Amen.
>
> —MATTHEW 6:9–13

It is actually an example of all three types of prayer—devotional prayer, intercessory prayer, and personal petition—but for the sake of simplicity we will consider it along with other forms of intercessory prayer. What a glorious gift it is to learn about prayer from the Man who had the greatest prayer life of all time!

How did this prayer come about? Jesus was on a hillside by the Sea of Galilee, teaching the multitudes and His disciples what it means to live a kingdom lifestyle according to His priorities, His heart, and His values. We know His teaching, recorded in Matthew 5–7, as the Sermon on the Mount, and I refer to it as the "constitution of God's kingdom." It was in this context that Jesus said to His followers, "In this manner, pray," and then gave them a model for prayer that provides insight into what God is like and into the nature of the kingdom and how it functions.

WHAT CAN I DO?

Ask the Father to help you pray as Jesus did—to keep your prayers focused, simple, yet powerful.

FOR REFLECTION

"Now it came to pass, as He was praying in a certain place, when He ceased, that one of His disciples said to Him, 'Lord, teach us to pray, as John also taught his disciples'" (Luke 11:1).

> *Father, teach and inspire us to pray in greater unity with Your heart. May Your kingdom come on earth—and in my life—as it is in heaven. I pray for a greater measure of peace to touch my mind and heart.*

_____

_____

_____

_____

_____

_____

_____

_____

_____

_____

_____

_____

_____

Day 53

Seeing God as Father and King

Before you intercede, be quiet first, and worship God.
Think of what He can do and how He delights to
hear the prayers of His people. Think of your place
and privilege in Christ, and expect great things!

—ANDREW MURRAY

IN HIS PRAYER to His Father, Jesus gave us keys that we need in our quest to grow strong in prayer. In essence He was saying, "Keep these things central in your prayer life." He gave us six requests to pray regularly, each with many implications and applications. The first three focus on *God's glory* (His name, kingdom, and will); the second three focus on *man's needs* (physical, relational, and spiritual).

Jesus' teaching on prayer begins by acknowledging God as our Father: "Our Father in heaven, hallowed be Your name" (Matt. 6:9). Here, at the beginning of His prayer, Jesus was showing them that their creator, God, is also their Father. He wanted them to see His affection, tenderness, and personal involvement with His people. Jesus emphasized both dimensions of God: His *majestic transcendence* as the One who dwells in heaven and His *tenderness as a father*. He is both powerful and personal, transcendent and tender.

We end up with a wrong view of God if we separate these two aspects of His nature. Throughout history the church has laid much emphasis on the transcendent God who rules with infinite power and has largely missed the tender father-heart of God. When the truth of the Father's heart of love comes into focus alongside His majestic splendor, we gain a more accurate picture of who God is.

Jesus started right where we need to start in our prayer lives, with our focus on the being of God Himself.

WHAT CAN I DO?

Reflect on God's kingship as you come into your sacred aloneness with the Father. Realize that He is both your Father whose heart is for you and your King who is over all the nations.

FOR REFLECTION

"O LORD, the God of our fathers, are You not God in the heavens? And are You not ruler over all the kingdoms of the nations? Power and might are in Your hand so that no one can stand against You" (2 Chron. 20:6).

> *Lord, Your majesty overwhelms me at times. Yet I am privileged to call You Abba Father, and know that You have a Father's heart toward me.*

_____

_____

_____

_____

_____

_____

_____

_____

_____

_____

Day 54

Praying for God's Glory

There is no power like that of prevailing prayer....It turns ordinary mortals into men of power. It brings power. It brings fire. It brings life. It brings God.

—Samuel Chadwick

In His prayer model Jesus gave us six requests to pray regularly. The first three requests are for God's glory—that His name be treated as holy, that His kingdom be openly expressed, and that His will be done individually and collectively by His people. Let's look at the first petition here: praying for God's name to be hallowed.

Our Father in heaven, hallowed be Your name.

—Matthew 6:9

God's name refers to His person, character, and authority. His name is hallowed when we respond to Him in the way He deserves. The very thought of His name stirs awe and holy fear in any who have a little understanding. This first petition is that God's majestic name be revealed first *to* us and then *through* us.

When we pray for His name to be hallowed, we are praying that the Father take the highest place in our lives, hearts, and worship, and that He work in us and in others so that we see and respond appropriately to His greatness. We are asking God to release His power to cause more people to see the truth about Him and refuse to take His name in vain or use it in jest and expressions of anger. We also revere God's name by not asking for anything contrary to His glorious name or will.

WHAT CAN I DO?

Allow your heart to be filled with awe and holy fear as you think about God. Ask the Lord to give you an increase of the fear of the Lord that you may respond to Him accordingly.

FOR REFLECTION

"Teach me Your way, O LORD; I will walk in Your truth; Unite my heart to fear Your name" (Ps. 86:11).

Lord, release the spirit of the fear of the Lord in my heart in a greater way.

_____

_____

_____

_____

_____

_____

_____

_____

_____

_____

_____

_____

_____

_____

_____

_____

_____

Day 55

Praying for the Kingdom to Come

Beware in your prayers, above everything else, of limiting God, not only by unbelief, but by fancying that you know what He can do. Expect unexpected things "above all that you ask or think."

—Andrew Murray

THE SECOND PETITION in the Lord's Prayer is "Your kingdom come" (Matt. 6:10). The kingdom is the place where God's Word is obeyed, His will done, and His power expressed. For example, the kingdom is manifested when the sick are healed and demons are cast out. Jesus told us, "If I cast out demons by the Spirit of God, surely the kingdom of God has come upon you" (Matt. 12:28). The kingdom is present wherever God's will is expressed under the authority of Jesus the King.

The kingdom is the sphere in which God's rule is expressed, and the church is the family and the vehicle of the kingdom. The church is the community of the kingdom. As the church proclaims the good news of the kingdom, people come into the church, the body of Christ, and experience the blessings of God's kingdom rule.

The schoolteacher who does God's will in the classroom is expressing God's kingdom in that setting. The same is true of the one who works at the bank, the gas station, the hospital, or the courthouse. It is true for the surgeon, the ditch digger, the soldier, the homeschooling mom, and all those who do God's will. The kingdom is already here but not yet fully here. It is manifest *in part* in this age and will be manifest *in fullness* when Jesus returns to earth.

Praying for the release of the kingdom is part of the work of the kingdom. We must not allow our service in the kingdom to take the place of conversing with the King and praying for the kingdom to come. This second petition includes being kingdom-minded in our lifestyles and in our attitudes toward others. We are to work together with other believers rather than having a territorial mindset and focusing on only our own spheres of authority and influence.

WHAT CAN I DO?

Think about ways you can do God's will in your sphere of influence—at work, as you socialize with friends, in family gatherings, in targeted outreaches with your church. Get creative and listen to the Holy Spirit's promptings.

FOR REFLECTION

"But seek first the kingdom of God and His righteousness, and all these things shall be added to you" (Matt. 6:33).

> *Lord, help me to be kingdom-minded in my daily life and in my attitude toward others. Bring those who are hungry for the Truth across my path.*

_____

_____

_____

_____

_____

_____

_____

_____

Day 56

Praying for God's Will to Be Done

Intercession is the universal work for the
Christian. No place is closed to prayer. No nation
or organization or city or office. There is no
power on earth that can keep intercession out.

—RICHARD HALVERSON

THE THIRD REQUEST related to God's glory in the Lord's Prayer is that His people will do His will, both individually and collectively. (See Matthew 6:10.) In this prayer we set our hearts to obey His will. Obeying His will includes obeying His commands in our personal lives as well as fulfilling the ministry assignments He gives to each of us. We pray for God's will to be done *through* us (in our ministries) and *in* us (in our personal lives). Some believers are committed to changing the nations through ministry but not to living in purity; they are more captivated by growing their ministries as "agents for change" than by interacting with Jesus and obeying Him in their personal lives. However, there is no substitute for obedience and intimacy with God.

As we pray for the Father's will to be done on earth, for the outworking of His righteousness, holiness, and love in our personal lives and in our midst, we are mindful that His will is being done perfectly in heaven. We are praying that earth become more like heaven, where the righteous, humble King reigns in the perfection of love and all of heaven rejoices in His majestic beauty.

WHAT CAN I DO?

Set your heart to obey God's will and to desire it—as much as He does. Notice how forming a habit of obedience transforms you by degrees into Christlikeness.

FOR REFLECTION

"And do not be conformed to this world, but be transformed by the renewing of your mind, that you may prove what *is* that good and acceptable and perfect will of God" (Rom. 12:2).

> *Heavenly Father, teach me to want what You want, to love what You love, and to be a vessel of godliness. I pray that Your will be done in me and through the churches in my city.*

_____

_____

_____

_____

_____

_____

_____

_____

_____

_____

_____

_____

_____

_____

Day 57

Daily Bread: Our Physical Needs

*The little estimate we put on prayer is
evidence from the little time we give to it.*

—E. M. BOUNDS

THIS FOURTH REQUEST in the Lord's Prayer—"Give us this day our daily bread" (Matt. 6:11)—is for our daily provision, protection, and direction. We do not pray to inform God of our needs, because He knows them before we ask (Matt. 6:7–8). Rather, we pray to enhance our relationship with Him by connecting and dialoguing with Him. Though He already knows our needs, He often withholds some of our provision until we talk to Him about it by making requests in prayer.

Asking God to meet our needs does not free us from the responsibility of working. He meets our needs partially by giving us the ability and opportunity to earn a living. But He delights in meeting all our needs because He is our Father.

Please note that Jesus taught us to ask for our "daily" bread. Most of us would prefer for the Lord to give us monthly bread or yearly bread, but He promised to give us bread only one day at a time.

WHAT CAN I DO?

Think of a time when you would have much preferred God give you "yearly bread." Then consider why His way—giving you *daily* bread— is the better way to be strengthened in your relationship with God and to develop your character.

FOR REFLECTION

"Don't worry and say, 'What will we eat?' or 'What will we drink?' or 'What will we wear?' That's what those people who don't know God are always thinking about. Don't worry, because your Father in heaven knows that you need all these things" (Matt. 6:31–32, ERV).

> *Lord, thank You in advance for providing all my daily needs. You know even before I ask just what I need. Lord, I thank You that You know me better than I know myself and delight in meeting the needs of Your people! Father, increase my understanding of Your timing and help me to learn to trust more in Your leadership. Thank You for having my best interest in mind.*

Day 58

Father, Forgive Us

Prayer is the language of a man
burdened with a sense of need.

—E. M. Bounds

THE FIFTH PETITION in the Lord's Prayer is to "forgive us our debts, as we forgive our debtors" (Matt. 6:12). The evidence that we have been freely forgiven is that we gladly forgive others. The man who knows he has been forgiven is compelled to forgive others.

Because Jesus is speaking to believers here, the question is often asked, "Why must a born-again believer pray for forgiveness?" When we ask God to "forgive us our debts," we are not asking to be saved or delivered from hell. We have already been freely forgiven and justified by faith (Rom. 3:21–31). Prayer for our debts to be forgiven speaks of restoring our fellowship with God. The apostle John explained this principle clearly in his first letter (1 John 1:8–9).

We do not lose our standing with God when, as sincere believers, we stumble in sin, but sin defiles our minds and quenches our hearts, thus hindering our ability to enjoy the presence of God. So we understand that this petition to "forgive us our debts" is to restore communion with Jesus. Again, John tells us, "If anyone sins, we have an Advocate with the Father, Jesus Christ the righteous" (1 John 2:1). This fifth petition is asking that we would be cleansed from the defiling effects of sin on our hearts.

Some believers have misinterpreted the second part of this petition, "as we forgive our debtors," to mean that we earn our forgiveness on the basis of forgiving others. That is not at all what Jesus is saying here. Rather, the evidence that we have been freely forgiven is that we are compelled by gratitude to extend that forgiveness to others.

WHAT CAN I DO

Make a list of people you need to forgive, including yourself if that applies. Bring your list before God in prayer and name each person as you forgive them. Ask the Lord to keep you from recycling old offenses, and consider it done.

FOR REFLECTION

"If we say that we have no sin, we deceive ourselves, and the truth is not in us. If we confess our sins, He is faithful and just to forgive us our sins and to cleanse us from all unrighteousness" (1 John 1:8–9).

Father, I remember Your faithfulness in my life and ask that You forgive me for sinning against You. Restore a sweet communion between us. Help me and teach me how to walk out deep forgiveness toward those who have hurt me. Father, I pray that You would heal my heart and help me by the Spirit to fully forgive and release them. Let it start today! In Jesus' name.

Day 59

Deliverance From Evil

*Oh brother, pray; in spite of Satan, pray;
spend hours in prayer; rather neglect
friends than not pray; rather fast, and lose
breakfast, tea, and supper—than not pray.*

—ANDREW A. BONAR

THE SIXTH PETITION in the Lord's Prayer—"And lead us not into temptation, but deliver us from the evil one" (Matt. 6:13, NIV)—is what I refer to as a "pre-temptation prayer." Jesus called us to pray for the Lord's help to avoid and escape "intensified" temptations before they even occur. This is a very important prayer, yet it may be one of the most neglected prayers in the Bible. In it Jesus expressed one petition in two ways: "lead us not into temptation" and "deliver us from evil." The second half of the request defines positively what the first half expresses negatively.

God never tempts anyone with evil (James 1:13), so why ask Him to "lead us not into temptation"? In the Garden of Gethsemane, Jesus urged the disciples to pray that they would not enter into temptation: "Watch and pray, lest you enter into temptation. The spirit is willing, but the flesh is weak" (Matt. 26:41).

To "enter into temptation" is to fall into something far more intense than the general temptations we face each day in a fallen world. It points to a specific "storm of temptation" that occurs when three components come together—demonic activity is heightened, our lusts are aroused, and circumstances are "optimum" for sin. By praying, we can avoid or minimize the intensity of a heightened temptation.

I see Jesus' petition in the Lord's Prayer as being focused on escaping the storms of temptation, which include more than general temptations that occur in everyday life. I think of "general" temptations as temptations to be proud in our attitudes, lack patience in our communication styles, act selfishly in our decisions, and be less than honest with our finances or in our communication with others. I think of the "storm" of temptations as acts such as committing adultery or participating in activities that cause serious harm to others or to society itself. I see the most serious temptation as the temptation to deny Christ.

The Scripture tells us that after he tempted Jesus, Satan departed until a more "opportune time" (Luke 4:13). Satan always looks for opportune times when demonically energized temptations will hit us like a storm and cause us to fall in a great way. He seeks to lure us into a trap "at an opportune time" to destroy our faith.

"Pre-temptation prayers" ask the Lord for help in advance and remove or diminish a storm of temptation. Praying before temptation occurs expresses our humility because we are acknowledging our weakness and our dependence on God's strength when we ask Him to lead us away from various temptations so that we do not become trapped by them.

WHAT CAN I DO?

Stay away from activities and people that may present a snare of temptation for you. You know the ones. As the saying goes, better to be safe than sorry. Seek to better understand your weaknesses and what "triggers you" in a way that causes you to stumble. Ask the Lord for creative ways to avoid engaging with the people or activities that have resulted in you falling in the past.

FOR REFLECTION

"Watch and pray, lest you enter into temptation. The spirit is willing, but the flesh is weak" (Matt. 26:41).

Lord, I ask that You protect me today and keep me from temptation. Remove or diminish any storm of temptation the evil one plans to send my way.

Day 60

Laying Hold of Prophetic Promises

*Prayer is not overcoming God's reluctance
but laying hold of His willingness.*

—MARTIN LUTHER

THERE IS A dynamic relationship between prophetic promises and persevering prayer. As our faith is stirred by prophetic promises, we are energized to sustain our prayer for the full release of those promises. Indeed, prayer and the prophetic are inseparable. Prophetic promises fuel the work of intercession, purity, and more effective outreach to others. They help us persevere in our faith and obedience so that we do not draw back in times of pressure and difficulty.

Prophetic promises are often invitations rather than guarantees. God speaks prophetically to equip us to more fully cooperate with the Holy Spirit as we intercede for the full release of what God has promised.

We value prophetic promises especially from the Scriptures, but we should not neglect personal prophetic promises that are confirmed by the Holy Spirit. Paul exhorted Timothy to fight the fight of faith according to the prophetic words that were given to him: "This charge I commit to you, son Timothy, according to the prophecies previously made concerning you, that by them you may wage the good warfare" (1 Tim. 1:18). Prophetic words help us to persevere in faithfulness in our assignments from the Lord, especially difficult ones.

Remember, however, that the foundation of our ministry must be on Jesus and our relationship with Him as confirmed in the written Word of God. We do not base our ministry on personal prophetic words. We must never receive prophetic promises that do not honor the written Word or that contradict it. The Scriptures are the final authority on all matters of faith, including prophetic promises. All contemporary or personal prophecies must be confirmed by the Spirit through two or three witnesses (2 Cor. 13:1).

WHAT CAN I DO?

Write down any prophetic promises you have received and prayerfully ask God to stir your faith for their fulfillment.

FOR REFLECTION

"He [Abraham] did not waver at the promise of God through unbelief, but was strengthened in faith, giving glory to God, and being fully convinced that what He had promised He was also able to perform" (Rom. 4:20–21).

Lord, help me to persevere in prayer as I wait for the fulfillment of Your prophetic promises to me. Stir up my faith! I set my heart to contend for all the prophetic promises over my life. I ask that You increase my faith as I pray and contend for them in my life.

Day 61

Biblical Promises for a Great Outpouring

Until we know that life is war, we won't know what prayer is for.

—JOHN PIPER

I AM CONVINCED THAT the greatest outpouring of the Holy Spirit in all of history will be released just before Jesus' second coming. The body of Christ will participate in the greatest revival ever to occur in the generation in which the Lord returns. In this great revival the Holy Spirit will release the types of miracles recorded in Acts and Exodus, combined and multiplied on a global scale.

How do I know? Because the Bible contains many promises related to the end times. And it tells us that Jesus is coming back for a glorious church that walks in holiness without any blemish or compromise (Eph. 5:27).

Biblical promises confirm that the body of Christ worldwide can expect to witness various expressions of revival in the end times. I will identify five:

+ We will see the emergence of a victorious, unified, anointed church that is full of God's glory. (See Jesus' prayer in John 17:22–23.)

+ The church will live in love, humility, and purity as a bride who is fully prepared for the Lord by living according to Jesus' Sermon on the Mount (Matt. 5–7).

✦ We will see a great end-time harvest from every nation, tribe, and tongue. I expect this great ingathering of souls to exceed one billion new souls coming to Jesus.

I looked, and behold, a great multitude which no one could number, of all nations, tribes, peoples, and tongues, standing before the throne and before the Lamb.... "These are the ones who come out of the great tribulation, and washed their robes and made them white in the blood of the Lamb."

—REVELATION 7:9, 14

✦ The spirit of prophecy will operate in the church and rest on every believer.

And it shall come to pass in the last days, says God, that I will pour out of My Spirit on all flesh; your sons and your daughters shall prophesy, your young men shall see visions, your old men shall dream dreams.

—ACTS 2:17

✦ The body of Christ will fulfill its primary calling to make disciples as we win the lost and to build His church—a kingdom community expressing the two great commandments to love God and people and fully engaging in the Great Commission.

Go therefore and make disciples of all the nations...teaching them to observe all things that I have commanded you.

—MATTHEW 28:19–20

We must embrace a tension as we contend in prayer for the full release of these prophetic promises of revival: we are to operate in a *partial* release of God's power *now* while also continuing to earnestly pray for a historic breakthrough of the *fullness* of the Spirit.

WHAT CAN I DO?

Ask the Lord how He can use you in fulfilling His purposes on earth. Make yourself available to Him, and listen for His leading.

FOR REFLECTION

"That He might present her to Himself a glorious church, not having spot or wrinkle or any such thing, but that she should be holy and without blemish" (Eph. 5:27).

> *Father, I join my faith to the faith of my brothers and sisters in Christ as we contend for a full release of Your prophetic promises for revival. We agree with heaven for a historic breakthrough of the fullness of the Spirit.*

Day 62

An Encounter With God in a Cairo Hotel

Prayer gives work its worth and its success. Prayer opens the way for God to do His work in us and through us. Let our chief work as God's messengers be intercession; in it we secure the presence and power of God to go with us.

—ANDREW MURRAY

FOR MANY YEARS I read about the revivals that accompanied the ministry of heroes of the faith such as Jonathan Edwards, John Wesley, George Whitefield, David Brainerd, and Charles Finney. I read their teaching alongside that of Martyn Lloyd-Jones and the Puritan writers—those who had a grasp of the biblical promises about revival—and I adopted their theology of an unprecedented ingathering of souls at the end of the age.

Much later my confidence in an end-time outpouring of the Spirit became a very personal issue. One night in September 1982, in a rather shabby hotel room in Cairo, Egypt, I experienced a life-changing encounter in the Holy Spirit. The eight-by-eight-foot room was equipped with a small bed, squeaky ceiling fan, stone-age plumbing, and an assortment of crawling things that periodically scampered across the concrete floor. I was alone and had set aside the evening to spend with the Lord in prayer. I had been kneeling on the cement floor by the rickety bed for about thirty minutes when I suddenly had one of the most important encounters with the Lord that I've had in over forty-five years of walking with God.

I didn't see a vision, and I wasn't caught up into heaven. The Lord clearly spoke to me—not in an audible voice that I could perceive with my natural ears but in what I call the "internal audible voice" of the Lord. I was instantly overwhelmed with a sense of God's presence. It came with a powerful feeling of cleanness, power, and authority. The awe of God flooded my soul as I felt a bit of the terror of the Lord. I literally trembled and wept as God Himself communicated to me in a way I had never experienced before and have not experienced since.

The Lord simply said, *"I will change the understanding and expression of Christianity in the whole earth in one generation."* It was a simple, straightforward statement, but I felt God's power with every word as I received the Spirit's interpretation: God Himself will make drastic changes in Christianity across the whole world, and this reformation-revival will be by His sovereign initiative and for His glory.

I knew by the Holy Spirit that the phrase "the understanding of Christianity" meant the way Christianity is perceived by unbelievers. In the early church, people were afraid to associate casually with believers, partly because of the displays of supernatural power (Acts 5:13). Today most unbelievers consider the church antiquated and irrelevant to their lives. God is going to change the way unbelievers view the church. Once again they will witness God's wonderful yet terrifying power in His body. They will have a very different understanding of Christianity before God is finished with this generation.

WHAT CAN I DO?

Ask the Father what part you can play as He restores His church with displays of supernatural power. Be faithful to the Lord today in small things, knowing that He will use this to prepare you for greater things that will surely come. Read stories about revival to stir faith in your heart. I suggest authors like some of the ones I've mentioned already, including Charles Finney, John Wesley, Jonathan Edwards, George Whitefield, David Brainerd, and John G. Lake.

FOR REFLECTION

"And it shall come to pass afterward that I will pour out My Spirit on all flesh; your sons and your daughters shall prophesy, your old men shall dream dreams, your young men shall see visions. And also on *My* menservants and on *My* maidservants I will pour out My Spirit in those days" (Joel 2:28–29).

> *Lord, You've done it before, so do it again—pour out Your Spirit on the earth in an astounding way. Empower Your church to turn the world upside down again!*

Day 63

The Cairo Encounter, Part 2

*Secret, fervent, believing prayer lies at
the root of all personal godliness.*

—WILLIAM CAREY

As I mentioned in Day 62, during my visit to Cairo, Egypt, in 1982, I had an incredible encounter with the Holy Spirit in my hotel room one night. I heard the Lord say, *"I will change the understanding and expression of Christianity in the whole earth in one generation."* I knew by the Holy Spirit that the phrase "the expression of Christianity" meant the way the body of Christ expresses its life together under Jesus' leadership. God will bring about dramatic change so that we function as a unified, holy people in the power and love of God. What happens when we gather together as the body of Christ will change. We will see unparalleled power, purity, and unity in the end-time church.

God Himself will radically change Christians' relationships with God and with one another, the way we are perceived by unbelievers, and even the structure and functioning of the church across the whole earth. He will do it not in a month, a year, or a few years, but over a generation. He will use His people who are serving in many different denominations and ministry streams in the body of Christ. He loves the whole church and will use all who want to be used by Him.

The understanding and expression of Christianity will be changed by a great, sovereign outpouring of the Spirit that will cross national, social, ethnic, cultural, and denominational barriers. It won't be just a Western revival or a third-world revival. The prophecy in Joel

2:28–32, reiterated by Peter in Acts 2, says that in the last days God will pour out His Spirit on "all flesh" (v. 17).

Much will change as a result of the progressive outpouring of the Spirit. It will have multidimensional expressions so that it will be seen not as only one type of movement—an evangelism movement, a healing movement, a prayer movement, a unity movement, or a prophetic movement. It will be all of these and more. Above all, this outpouring of the Spirit will impart deep passion for Jesus in the hearts of men and women. The first commandment to love God will be established in first place in the church, which will lead to the church's walking in the second commandment to love others and engaging in the Great Commission in an unprecedented way. The Holy Spirit longs to glorify Jesus in the body of Christ throughout the nations. (See John 16:14.)

My experience in the Cairo hotel room lasted less than an hour, though it seemed longer. I left the room and walked around the streets of downtown Cairo alone until about midnight, committing myself to the Lord and His purposes. The awe of God lingered in my soul for hours. I woke up the next day still feeling its impact.

This experience gave me a new appreciation for the prophetic ministry, helping me realize that it is essential to "fueling" the end-time prayer movement. The prophetic ministry in the local church will involve more than verbal, inspirational prophecies. It will include angelic visitations, dreams, visions, signs and wonders in the sky, and more. The Holy Spirit will be poured out in great power and God's people will prophesy as foretold in Joel 2 and cited in Peter's first sermon on the Day of Pentecost.

WHAT CAN I DO?

Let God know you want to be used as He changes the expression and understanding of Christianity throughout the earth. Stand up and be counted among those who represent a church that is walking in the power of the Holy Spirit. Ask the Lord to give you more insight and faith in the commission that He gave to all of His people—to preach the gospel, heal the brokenhearted, and proclaim liberty to the captives (Luke 4:18).

FOR REFLECTION

"For I will pour water on him who is thirsty, and floods on the dry ground; I will pour My Spirit on your descendants, and My blessing on your offspring" (Isa. 44:3).

> *Heavenly Father, bring about such dramatic change in Your church that we function as a unified, holy people in the power and love of God. Fuel us for the end-time awakening that is already on the horizon.*

Day 64

Our Model for Spiritual Warfare

*Satan trembles when he sees the
weakest Christian on his knees.*

—WILLIAM COWPER

THE NEW TESTAMENT model for spiritual warfare is to *direct
our prayers to God*, proclaim His name and promises, and do
His works as the primary way to wrestle with the "disembodied"
evil spirits in the heavenly places. Thus, as a general rule, we speak
directly to God instead of addressing them directly. In my opinion
there are exceptions to this general rule, in which case we address
our proclamations directly to a demonic principality. However, this
is not the primary prayer model presented by the New Testament
apostles.

Jesus and the apostles spoke directly to the demons that dwelt
in a demonized person—in other words, to "embodied" demonic
spirits—but what they did is not the same as speaking to "disembodied" demonic principalities that dwell in heavenly places. We
do wrestle with disembodied demonic principalities (Eph. 6:12) but
usually by praying to the Father, not by speaking to them directly. ·
The prophet Daniel prevailed over the powerful demonic principality
of Persia (Dan. 10:12–13) as he fasted and prayed, focusing on the
God of Israel (Dan. 9:4–23), not on the demonic being itself.

I see three components involved in spiritual warfare prayers:

1. We proclaim God's victory in prayer by agreeing
   with the supremacy of Jesus, His power, promises,
   and will. We pray the prayers of the Bible, remind

God of His promises, and make prophetic decrees related to the supremacy of God and His kingdom purposes.

2. We confess sin and renounce the works of darkness, thus breaking our agreement with the enemy. As we resist Satan and submit to God and His Word, the devil flees from us (James 4:7).

3. We do the works of the kingdom, acting in the opposite spirit of the evil characteristics that permeate a specific city or region. For example, in a place where oppression is identified as a spiritual stronghold, the body of Christ should focus on doing acts of generosity, servanthood, and so on.

Over the next few days we will delve deeper into the topic of spiritual warfare. As Christians, we have victory over the enemy, and God wants us to live in that reality.

WHAT CAN I DO?

Keep your prayers focused on the Father, not on the evil one. Use the Word of God to speak back to Him "thy kingdom come" so that His will shall be done on earth as it is in heaven. Seek to discern more precisely when the enemy assaults you with lies, fear, and accusation. Speak the truths of God's Word to resist and combat lies.

FOR REFLECTION

"For we do not wrestle against flesh and blood, but against principalities, against powers, against the rulers of the darkness of this age, against spiritual hosts of wickedness in the heavenly places" (Eph. 6:12).

137

*Lord, help me to resist the evil one and submit to You today as
I proclaim Your name and declare Your truth.*

Day 65

Three Types of Strongholds

*We give too much attention to method and
machinery and resources, and too little to
the source of power through prayer.*

—Hudson Taylor

THE SCRIPTURE SPEAKS of pulling down spiritual "strongholds": "For the weapons of our warfare are not carnal but mighty in God for pulling down strongholds, casting down arguments and every high thing that exalts itself against the knowledge of God" (2 Cor. 10:4–5). A stronghold consists of a collection of ideas in agreement with Satan's lies and accusations against the truth of God (v. 5). They are lies about God, who He is, and what He says He will do, as well as lies about who we are in Christ and how He sees us, and when we receive the lies, they bind our hearts in darkness.

Whole geographic regions can be affected by the same lies and assaulted by the same demonic darkness. One way we can recognize this is that we see a large number of people in a region embracing the same patterns of darkness in their beliefs and behavior. We pull down and dismantle spiritual strongholds by agreeing with God and His Word and by "casting down arguments"—renouncing the lies—that are against the knowledge of God, His Word, and His will. In this way we break any agreement with Satan.

I will mention three types of spiritual strongholds:

+ *Personal strongholds* of the mind that bind people in sinful mind-sets and lifestyles.

+ *Cultural strongholds* are agreements with Satan's values in our society at large. There are many ways in which people agree with him and keep those values entrenched.

+ *Cosmic strongholds*, which are demonic powers and principalities in the air, are demonic angels or demonic hosts. Paul describes them in his letter to the Ephesians: "For we do not wrestle against flesh and blood, but against principalities, against powers, against the rulers of the darkness of this age, against spiritual hosts of wickedness in the heavenly places" (Eph. 6:12).

We should not let these strongholds intimidate us because we have the key to their undoing. We dismantle each of them by *agreeing* with God and *renouncing* the enemy's lies through our prayers and actions.

WHAT CAN I DO?

Pull down and dismantle spiritual strongholds over your life by agreeing with God and His Word, and by renouncing the lies of the evil one.

FOR REFLECTION

"Having disarmed principalities and powers, [Jesus] made a public spectacle of them, triumphing over them in it" (Col. 2:15).

> *Father, I dismantle every stronghold over my life and the lives of my loved ones by agreeing with You and renouncing the enemy's lies. Show me anywhere in my life where I have believed a lie and highlight areas where I have embraced wrong thinking.*

I will speak Your truth into these areas and pray for break-through and freedom in the name of Jesus!

_____

_____

_____

_____

_____

_____

_____

_____

_____

_____

_____

_____

_____

_____

_____

_____

_____

_____

_____

_____

_____

_____

_____

_____

_____

_____

_____

_____

Day 66

Drawing Back the Veil on the Spirit Realm

Many Christians...do their best to fight against sin, and to serve God, but they have never grasped the secret: Jesus from heaven continues His work in me on one condition— the soul must give Him time to impart His love and His grace. Time alone with Jesus is the indispensable condition of growth and power.

—ANDREW MURRAY

DANIEL 10 GIVES us a snapshot of what happens in the spirit realm when God's people pray. This is a favorite chapter for many intercessors because the veil is drawn back, allowing us to see how our prayers affect angels and demonic powers and principalities. It also reveals the intense conflict between high-ranking angels and demons that is manifest in earthly spheres of government.

Angelic and demonic authority structures exist over each city and region in the world. There are high-ranking angels that serve God's purposes, and there are high-ranking demons that fight His purposes. The conflict between these angelic and demonic beings is dynamically related to the prayers and deeds of the people in the city or region the beings preside over. If we could see into the spirit realm, I believe we would be amazed by how much the heavenly host is involved in earthly affairs and how they respond to our prayers.

There is a dynamic correlation between what people do on earth and the measure of demonic activity that is released in the areas in which they live. For example, as people sin more in a particular city or region, they give greater access to the demonic realm to increase the amount of spiritual darkness in that city or region. The same principle operates in the angelic realm—the righteous deeds and prayers of the saints affect the measure of angelic activity in a specific area.

When we pray, the Holy Spirit and the angels increase their activity on behalf of all those for whom we pray, and the result ultimately benefits us. Paul understood this truth, so he encouraged the body of Christ to make it a priority to pray for all in authority.

WHAT CAN I DO?

Pray for spiritual discernment and that God will open your spiritual eyes and ears so you can see and hear beyond your natural senses.

FOR REFLECTION

"Therefore I exhort first of all that supplications, prayers, intercessions, and giving of thanks be made for all men, for kings and all who are in authority, that we may lead a quiet and peaceable life in all godliness and reverence" (1 Tim. 2:1–2).

> *Lord, I ask that You send a greater measure of Your Spirit and Your holy angels to fight on behalf of righteousness and bring about Your purposes. I pray that there would be an increase of light and angelic activity in my home, my church, and in my city.*

Day 67

Learning From Daniel's Example

If you believe in prayer at all, expect God to hear you.
—CHARLES SPURGEON

WHEN THE PROPHET Daniel was probably in his mideighties, he set his heart to pray for the Jews in Jerusalem. He prayed for twenty-one days, mourning with prayer and fasting because of the resistance of the remnant back in Jerusalem. In response to Daniel's prayer a mighty angel came and said to Daniel:

> From the first day that you set your heart to...humble yourself before your God, your words were heard; and I have come because of your words. But the prince [demonic principality] of the kingdom of Persia withstood me twenty-one days; and behold, Michael, one of the chief princes [archangel], came to help me.
>
> —DANIEL 10:12–13

The mighty angel made a dramatic statement: "I came because of your words." This statement makes clear that angels respond to the prayers of the saints. Gabriel had told Daniel the same thing two years earlier: "Because of your words, the Father sent me." (See Daniel 9:22–23.)

But if Daniel had not *continued* in prayer with fasting, the angel would not have come. It was important for Daniel to persevere in prayer for the full twenty-one days to get the necessary breakthrough. His experience proves that there is a dynamic relationship between what we do and how God visits a city or nation. Remember, this is not about "earning" anything but about aligning with Him by coming into *agreement* with His will. Our words are heard because of Jesus' death and resurrection.

Daniel fought the demonic prince of Persia by agreeing with God in prayer and fasting. The mighty angel informed him that "Michael, one of the chief princes, came to help" (Dan. 10:13). A "chief prince" is an archangel, one who leads angels.

Jesus can easily overpower a demonic principality. However, His authority is exerted or made manifest in the earthly realm through believers who agree with Him and who persevere in obedience and prayer with faith. The reason Jesus releases His power more through prayer is because He wants partnership with His people, and prayer is one of the main ways that partnership is strengthened.

The spiritual events of Daniel 10 were recorded in the Scripture to give us a model of what God wants to do in our day to hinder the demonic principalities over nations. These principalities can be withstood as the Spirit raises up a "corporate Daniel" to pray for angelic help to overcome the demonic powers assaulting Israel. Indeed, Daniel 10 is a model of spiritual warfare for the end-time church. Let us take our stand before the throne of God as we follow this prayer model and ask for angelic intervention in our world today.

WHAT CAN I DO?

Set your heart to pray for specific requests for which you earnestly desire to see a breakthrough. If you feel a prompting to fast and pray, consider doing a Daniel fast with set times of prayer each day.

FOR REFLECTION

"Then he said to me, 'Do not fear, Daniel, for from the first day that you set your heart to understand, and to humble yourself before your God, your words were heard; and I have come because of your words'" (Dan. 10:12).

Lord, I align myself with Your Word and Your will right now and ask You to release heavenly messengers to accomplish on earth what You have already declared in heaven.

Lifestyle of an Effective Intercessor

When God gets ready to do something new with
His people, He always sets them a-praying.

—EDWIN ORR

WOULD YOU LIKE your prayers to move angels and demons as Daniel's did? Would you like to experience similar results when you intercede? If we want a greater level of effectiveness in prayer along the lines of what Daniel had, we must live as he lived.

So what does the lifestyle of an effective intercessor look like? We will not really understand the message related to prayer in Daniel 10 without understanding Daniel's dedication to God. His lifestyle was directly related to his effectiveness in prayer. We must consider his dedication, especially his *consistency in prayer* throughout his life (Dan. 6:10); his determination to set his heart to walk in *wholehearted obedience* to God (Dan. 1:8); and his commitment to gain *understanding of God's will* for his generation (Dan. 10:12).

It is important to understand that Daniel's life of faithfulness did not earn God's power or greater effectiveness in prayer; rather, it positioned Daniel to live in greater agreement with God, and it was this agreement that impacted the effectiveness of his prayers. But the Old Testament is not the only place we find examples of effective prayer. The New Testament also has much to say about the quality of our lifestyles and their relationship to effective prayer. The essence of real faith is agreement with God—in our words, hearts, *and* lifestyles.

Daniel's prayers were offered by a man who was weak in the flesh just as we are. But through the blood of Jesus and our agreement with God, our prayers offered in weakness ascend to the throne of God in power just as Daniel's did.

Over the next few days, we will take a closer look at each of these three characteristics that marked Daniel's lifestyle.

WHAT CAN I DO?

Determine before God that you will be consistent in prayer, quick to obey, and set to understand His will. Ask the Holy Spirit to keep you accountable and remind you when you get off course. Ask the Lord to show you anything that is a hindrance to your life in prayer. They don't always have to be big "black-and-white" sin issues. Sometimes it is the little foxes that spoil the vine (Song of Sol. 2:15), the small gray areas that we say yes to.

FOR REFLECTION

"In his upper room, with his windows open toward Jerusalem, [Daniel] knelt down on his knees three times that day, and prayed and gave thanks before his God, as was his custom since early days" (Dan. 6:10).

> *Lord, I want to be a man/woman of prayer, consistent about meeting with You and obedient the very first time I hear a word. Teach me to understand Your will and walk in Your ways. Give me the grace to remove everything that may hinder breakthrough in my life and in the lives of others. May I see everything I do in light of Your truth.*

Day 69

Consistency in Prayer

*We only learn to behave ourselves
in the presence of God.*

—C. S. Lewis

ONE OF THE great miracles of Daniel's life was his consistency in prayer for more than sixty years. He had begun praying in his youth, probably in his teen years. If you are a young person reading this, I encourage you to follow Daniel's example and begin, or continue, having regular prayer times. You may be in your later years and regret the many years you have wasted, spiritually speaking, and think it is too late to start. But I have good news for you. It is never too late to start! We can begin today and make it our custom to be faithful in prayer for the rest of our days.

I think of the setbacks or disappointments that a young person often has in his or her twenties and thirties. Daniel suffered the same setbacks. The details were different, but the general disappointments surely were the same as those of other young people in other nations and in other generations. He refused to be offended by what God "did not do" for him in his young adult years or to become bitter toward those who mistreated or betrayed him, and he refused to be distracted from his prayer life by the great amount of work that came his way due to the rapid promotions in his political career.

Oh, the miracle of a life that stays consistent in seeking the Lord for decades in the face of the positive and negative experiences in life we all have! He must have said a million times, "No, I will not get off course; I will stay consistent in my prayer life."

I have no doubt that Daniel also faced pressures and opportunities in his fifties and sixties. It is easy for well-meaning, middle-aged believers to drift away from the commitment they made about their relationships with Jesus and specifically their prayer lives in their youths.

But despite the setbacks, resistance, pleasures, growing responsibilities, or wonderful opportunities throughout the years, Daniel remained steady in prayer. His consistency is one of the primary reasons he had such an effective prayer life in his eighties. It is also one of the reasons God used him as an example of a righteous, faithful intercessor.

WHAT CAN I DO?

Think about the setbacks and disappointments you have faced in your spiritual walk. Now look again with a "bigger picture" view of how God has kept you—and worked things out for your good when they looked like nothing good could possibly come from them.

FOR REFLECTION

"Then Daniel said to the king, 'O king, live forever! My God sent His angel and shut the lions' mouths, so that they have not hurt me, because I was found innocent before Him; and also, O king, I have done no wrong before you'" (Dan. 6:21–22).

> *Father, I am encouraged that it is never too late to start again with You. I want to be a faithful pray-er just like Daniel was. Help me in my weakness, and encourage me when I fall. Teach me how to be consistent in my obedience to You. Help me recommit to obey You, for as Your mercies are new every morning so is Your heart toward me. I thank You that You are for me!*

Wholehearted Obedience

*We can do nothing without prayer. All
things can be done by importunate prayer.
That is the teaching of Jesus Christ.*

—E. M. BOUNDS

THE RECORD OF Daniel's story in Scripture begins when Daniel was in his teen years. In those early days he purposed not to defile himself related to food or any pleasures: "But Daniel purposed in his heart that he would not defile himself with the portion of the king's delicacies, nor with the wine which he drank" (Dan. 1:8). The main point is not what specific food he avoided but that he determined to walk in wholehearted obedience in the face of peer pressure. He saw the lifestyle of other young people around him, but he made the choice not to live the way other young people lived.

Whether you are young or old, it is not too late to start. It is never too late to start. We can set our hearts to walk in wholehearted obedience beginning today. I encourage you to make that choice and to set your heart not to be defiled by food, immorality, porn, slander, lying about finances, or any other sin; and not to be too busy to spend time with God.

Daniel set his heart to not be defiled all his days. I am sure at the end of his life, when he stood before God, he had no regrets about giving up various pleasures. I am confident that he did not wish he had spent more time in recreation. On the last day when we all stand before Jesus, no one will regret having spent too little time playing video games or watching movies.

WHAT CAN I DO?

Make a list of pleasures you can "fast" from over the next week or month to make more room in your life for God. Do this as an expression of your love for Him. Remember that you are not earning anything, but expressing your own love for Him in a practical way.

FOR REFLECTION

"An excellent spirit, knowledge, understanding, interpreting dreams...were found in this Daniel....Then Daniel was brought in before the king. The king spoke, and said to Daniel, 'Are you that Daniel...? I have heard of you, that the Spirit of God is in you, and that light and understanding and excellent wisdom are found in you'" (Dan. 5:12–14).

Lord, like Daniel, I set my heart to not be defiled and to walk in an excellent spirit, being obedient to Your Word and Your will.

_____

_____

_____

_____

_____

_____

_____

_____

_____

_____

Day 71

Beloved of the Lord

Time spent alone with God is not wasted. It
changes our surroundings, and every Christian
who would live the life that counts, and who would
have power for service must take time to pray.

—M. E. Andross

THE LORD REVEALED His love to Daniel in a deep way through an angel, who addressed Daniel as the beloved of the Lord: "He [an angel] said to me, 'O Daniel, man greatly beloved...'" (Dan. 10:11).

Imagine a high-ranking angel telling you, "The Lord greatly loves you, and you are beloved by your God"; in other words, "The Lord is moved by the way you live. He is moved by your hunger for Him and by your lifestyle choices."

We know that God loves the world. He loves unbelievers, even though He does not enjoy a relationship with them. But there are those in whom God takes special delight; that is, He delights in the choices they make for Him. Jesus taught that the Father loves all who obey Him. He loves the relationship He has with all who keep His commandments, and He loves their life choices.

Jesus made the amazing statement that He would manifest Himself to those who show their love for Him in their words, actions, and lifestyles. No one is "good enough" to deserve a greater manifestation of God's glory. It's not about being good enough but about positioning ourselves to receive more from God.

Every believer can have a close relationship with the Lord. Daniel was forcibly taken to Babylon as a prisoner of war in his youth. Yet even as a captive, far from his home in Jerusalem and in a foreign culture, he determined to seek God with all his heart for all his days. Today the Lord is looking for men and women like Daniel, who will set their hearts to live before God as Daniel did. Daniel remained steady in His love for God and lived out his commitment in his daily life until he died.

In my forty-plus years of ministry I have seen many people go hard after God for five or even ten years. Most of them were young and in their twenties. By the time they reached thirty-five, several had "good" reasons for drawing back and being more "practical." I have seen only a few people stay consistent in seeking God with diligence for twenty or thirty years or more. Daniel stayed consistent in seeking God for sixty years, even during his time in the pagan city of Babylon.

I want the Lord to say to me on the last day, "I loved the way you spent your time and money and the way you obeyed Me; I loved the way that you loved Me." I want Him to be able to say the things about me that He said about Daniel. I want to be steady like this great man of God, even when I'm eighty. What about you?

WHAT CAN I DO?

Ask the Father to hem you in and keep your heart fervent before Him all the days of your life so that you too can be said to have gone "hard after God" when the story of your life is complete.

FOR REFLECTION

"But you have carefully followed my doctrine, manner of life, purpose, faith, longsuffering, love, perseverance" (2 Tim. 3:10).

> *Father, may I live in such a way that others—and even angels—will say of me, "The Lord is moved by the way you live. He is moved by your hunger for Him and by your lifestyle*

choices." I pray that I would carry my heart in such a way that
You find delight in the way I live and the choices I make.

_____

_____

_____

_____

_____

_____

_____

_____

_____

_____

_____

_____

_____

_____

_____

_____

_____

_____

_____

_____

_____

_____

_____

_____

_____

_____

_____

Prayers to Strengthen
Our Inner Man

We are too busy to pray, and so we are too busy
to have power. We have a great deal of activity,
but we accomplish little; many services but few
conversions; much machinery but few results.

—R. A. TORREY

IN HIS LETTER to the Ephesians the apostle Paul wrote the following prayer: "I bow my knees to the Father...that He would grant you...to be strengthened with might through His Spirit in the inner man" (Eph. 3:14–16).

The term *inner man* refers to a person's soul—one's mind, emotions, and will. It is where we are most aware of our interaction with the Holy Spirit. Our highest calling in life is our fellowship with God, and what happens in our inner man is an essential aspect of that fellowship. Therefore, our inner man is the most important part of us.

Prayer for our inner man includes growing in intimacy with Jesus—focusing on giving our love and devotion to God. This kind of prayer encompasses worship, fellowshipping with the Holy Spirit, and pray-reading the Word—including appropriating the names of God.

Just as our physical strength can increase or decrease, so can our experience of spiritual strength. We cannot always discern the specific times when the Spirit strengthens us; He usually does so in small measures. I compare being strengthened in our inner man to being strengthened by taking vitamins. Many of us have taken vitamins for years but cannot remember the precise day when we realized they were making a difference. However, we know that if we consistently take vitamins, they will strengthen us physically over time. It is the same with our inner man. If we ask regularly, the Spirit will release His might in our inner man (our mind, emotions, and will), and over time we will experience newfound strength. This divine strengthening of our hearts equips us to live in a godly way and enables us to stand against compromise, depression, fear, rejection, spiritual lethargy, and other negative emotions and behaviors.

Just as we must be intentional about taking vitamins, so we must be intentional about praying for the strengthening and development of our hearts in God. We will experience more of God's grace that renews our minds and emotions if we ask for it on a regular basis. I want to emphasize again the simple truth I mentioned earlier—God releases more blessing if we ask for it. In James 4:2 we are told, "You do not have because you do not ask." The Lord knows that we have needs, but He withholds many things until we ask Him.

WHAT CAN I DO?

Ask the Lord to strengthen you with spiritual might in your inner man. Make time for worship, fellowshipping with the Holy Spirit, and pray-reading the Word. When you read through the Scriptures in this way, they will come alive to you.

FOR REFLECTION

"That He would grant you, according to the riches of His glory, to be strengthened with might through His Spirit in the inner man" (Eph. 3:16).

> *Lord, strengthen my heart and equip me to live in a godly way today; enable me to stand against compromise, depression,*

fear, rejection, and spiritual lethargy. Lord, strengthen me with might in my inner man that I be strengthened in the very place of my weaknesses. I thank You for touching my heart with Your power. I delight in my need of You!

_____

_____

_____

_____

_____

_____

_____

_____

_____

_____

_____

_____

_____

_____

_____

_____

_____

_____

_____

_____

_____

_____

Day 73

Fellowshipping With the Holy Spirit

*The main lesson about prayer is just
this: Do it! Do it! Do it!*

—JOHN LAIDLAW

THE HOLY SPIRIT is a dynamic Person who lives inside our spirits. We are to fellowship, or commune, with Him by talking with Him often. We must deeply value and cultivate our friendship with the Spirit in an intentional way. One way to do this is by speaking to Him as the God who dwells within us. Some refer to this activity as abiding prayer, contemplative prayer, communing prayer, centering prayer, or the prayer of quiet.

A vibrant walk with the Spirit is essential in our quest to experience more of God. It is futile to seek deep experiences with God while neglecting the Spirit's leadership and relationship in our lives. We cannot go deep in God with a dull spirit. It is a glorious privilege for every believer to be able to fellowship with the Holy Spirit to the degree that He desires to.

Our greatest destiny is to grow in intimacy with God through the indwelling Spirit and thus share in the "family dynamics" of the Trinity. We are incredibly blessed that God has so opened His heart and family life to His people so that we may have deep fellowship with Him. This is the essence of Christianity and of true prayer.

Many think of prayer mostly in terms of seeking God's help to solve their problems, to gain more blessings in their circumstances, or to meet their needs related to sickness, finances, unsaved family members, loneliness, fear, guilt, relational conflicts, and so on. But there is so much more to growing in prayer than making requests to meet our needs! Prayer is first and foremost a call to communion with God by the indwelling Spirit.

WHAT CAN I DO?

Take time to read John 14–17 and be more intentional to talk to the Holy Spirit about many things, including His desire to teach and help you.

FOR REFLECTION

"May the grace of the Lord Jesus Christ, and the love of God, and the fellowship of the Holy Spirit be with you all" (2 Cor. 13:14, NIV).

> *Lord, help me to grow intimate with You through the indwelling Holy Spirit. Sharpen my spiritual senses so that I am keenly aware of Your abiding presence every moment of the day. Holy Spirit, I want to know and encounter You more. I thank You that it is Your joy to make known the glory of Jesus. Today, I ask that You teach me more about Jesus.*

Day 74

Walking With the Holy Spirit

> *Out of a very intimate acquaintance with [D.*
> *L. Moody] I wish to testify that he was a far*
> *greater pray-er than he was preacher. Time and*
> *time again, he was confronted by obstacles that*
> *seemed insurmountable, but he always knew the*
> *way...to overcome all difficulties....He knew and*
> *believed...that "nothing was too hard for the Lord,"*
> *and that prayer could do anything that God could do.*
>
> —R. A. TORREY

IN GALATIANS 5 Paul exhorted us to walk in the Spirit, which we do primarily by developing a dynamic friendship with Him, and then immediately gave us one of the great promises in Scripture, "you shall not fulfill the lust of the flesh."

> I say then: Walk in the Spirit, and you shall not fulfill the lust [sinful desires] of the flesh. For the flesh lusts [wars] against the Spirit, and the Spirit against the flesh.
>
> —GALATIANS 5:16–17

In Galatians 5:17 Paul described the war inside every believer: the flesh wars against the Spirit, and the Spirit wars against the flesh. The "flesh" in Paul's theology includes sinful pleasures (sensuality, gluttony, alcoholism, and so on) and sinful emotions (pride, bitterness, anger, defensiveness, and so on). In all, he identified seventeen expressions of the flesh. Paul did not promise us that all fleshly desires would be gone; he said we would have the power to avoid yielding to them and stumbling in them.

The only way to overcome the power of sinful desires is to grow in our relationship with the Holy Spirit by being actively engaged with Him. In other words, walking in the Spirit is the primary condition for overcoming these desires. The Spirit will war against them if we engage with the indwelling Spirit in a personal way. He will go to battle with power against our fleshly desires.

The way to walk in the Spirit is by fellowshipping with the Spirit. It is as simple as can be. *We walk in the Spirit to the degree that we talk to the Holy Spirit.* When was the last time you talked to the Holy Spirit as a person living in your spirit? We are to set our minds on Him and speak to Him directly (Rom. 8:6).

We will not *walk* in the Spirit more than we *talk* to the Spirit. This is so critical to understand and practice. Actually we will not *obey* Him more than we talk to Him. My understanding of what Jesus said in John 15:5 is, "Apart from connectedness with Me— abiding in Me—you cannot do *anything*."

He will not force us into the conversation, but if we talk to Him, He will "talk back." Once we begin the conversation, He will continue it as long we as we do. He speaks to us by giving us subtle impressions that release His power on our minds and hearts.

The more we talk to the Spirit, the less we talk to people in a way that quenches the Holy Spirit, our spirits, or their spirits.

WHAT CAN I DO?

Talk to the Spirit so you can walk with the Spirit. Notice all the small ways He's showing up in your life when you include Him in your daily inward conversations.

FOR REFLECTION

"Let no corrupt word proceed out of your mouth, but what is good for necessary edification, that it may impart grace to the hearers. *And do not grieve the Holy Spirit*" (Eph. 4:29–30).

Lord, help me to stay connected to You. May my relationship with You grow stronger and deeper even as my flesh grows weaker and weaker.

Talking to the Holy Spirit

*Prayer is the first thing, the second thing, the third
thing necessary to a minister...: pray, pray, pray.*

—EDWARD PAYSON

THE SPIRIT LONGS for us to talk with Him, but He will not force conversation or friendship on those who are not interested. When we talk to Him, He will talk back to us. Often when He "talks," He does not use words but rather gives us impressions, sensitizes our emotions so we can feel His nearness, or speaks through His Word. God leads us by the still, small voice in our inner man—the same still, small voice He used to speak to Elijah in 1 Kings 19:11–13.

Sadly, many believers do not talk to the indwelling Holy Spirit, thus depriving themselves of a most precious relationship. Saint Augustine testified that he lost much time seeking the Lord outwardly instead of turning inward. One of my favorite prayers—the one I use most often—is asking the Spirit to let me see what He sees and feel what He feels about my life, my family, and other people, as well as what He sees and feels about Jesus, the church, the great harvest, the nations, the end times, and so on.

Be intentional about talking to the Spirit—start by setting time aside three to five times each day (aim for three to five minutes each time). If we talk to the Spirit only when we are tempted, rather than as a lifestyle, we will not sustain our dialogue with Him in a way that results in our being changed. At first it may be difficult to bring your mind to focus on the indwelling Spirit. As you do it more often, you will become accustomed to withdrawing inwardly to speak to the Spirit. If your mind wanders, simply turn it back to the indwelling Spirit again.

In dialoguing with the indwelling Spirit, take time to linger, speaking slowly to Him. Include declarations of your love for Him. Speak slowly, with occasional whispers of "I love You, Holy Spirit," while intermittently praying in the Spirit. We practice the presence of God, knowing that it takes time to grow in our sense of connectedness with the indwelling Spirit. The more I speak directly to Him in private, the more I sense His presence in my public life with others.

WHAT CAN I DO?

Attune your spiritual ears for the still, small voice. Expect God to speak, and actively listen for His "internal audible voice."

FOR REFLECTION

"The Spirit of God dwells in you...Christ is in you...the Spirit is life because of righteousness" (Rom. 8:9–10).

Father, I desire to linger in Your presence right now. My heart and the "ears" of my spirit are open. Speak to me, Lord.

Day 76

T-R-U-S-T

*I have seen many men work without praying... but
I have never seen a man pray without working.*

—Hudson Taylor

I REGULARLY USE FIVE simple phrases to focus my conversation with the indwelling Spirit. The five-letter acronym
T-R-U-S-T helps me remember the phrases.

T: THANK YOU

The first thing we do is turn our attention inward to recognize the
Holy Spirit's presence and simply thank Him for His indwelling
presence.

Scripture

> He who abides in Me, and I in him, bears much fruit; for
> without Me you can do nothing.
>
> —John 15:5

Prayer

> *Thank You, Holy Spirit, for Your bright presence in me. I love
> Your presence. Apart from You, I can do nothing.*

R: RELEASE REVELATION OF YOUR GLORY

I ask the Spirit to release revelation of the realm of God's glory and
heart. Paul saw Jesus and His glory in a great light from heaven on
the day of his conversion. Moses prayed, "Please, show me Your glory"
(Exod. 33:18). Afterward his face shone with the light of glory. Like
Moses, we can ask to encounter the realm of God's glory.

Scripture

Suddenly a great light from heaven shone around me....And since I could not see for the glory of that light, being led by the hand of those who were with me, I came into Damascus.

—ACTS 22:6, 11

Prayer

Holy Spirit, open my eyes to see the realm of God's glory and to encounter His heart. I ask You to release revelation of Your glory to me. Allow me to see the glory and beauty of Jesus as Paul did.

U: USE ME

Paul exhorted us to seek diligently to be used in the gifts of the Holy Spirit (1 Cor. 12:31). The Spirit will use us more if we ask Him to.

Scripture

The manifestation of the Spirit is given to each one for the profit of all.

—1 CORINTHIANS 12:7

Prayer

Thank You for Your gifts. Release them in me in a greater measure, for the Word says that each person is given manifestation of the Spirit. Holy Spirit, release the manifestation of Your gifts and power through me to help others. I desire to be a vessel of Your presence to glorify Jesus.

S: STRENGTHEN ME

The Spirit will strengthen our inner man by touching our minds, emotions, and speech with the might of His presence. Because the

Spirit lives in us, the fruit of the Spirit—love, joy, peace, and so on—is in our spirits now. Thus, we can experience more of the power of this fruit by thanking Him that it is already in us.

Scripture

> That He would grant you, according to the riches of His glory, to be strengthened with might through His Spirit in the inner man.
>
> —EPHESIANS 3:16

Prayer

> *Holy Spirit, release divine might to strengthen my mind and emotions. Thank You for Your love, peace, and patience, which are already at work in me.*

T: TEACH ME

The indwelling Spirit is the great teacher who is committed to lead us into God's will and ways so that we are able to live in deep partnership with Him. Ask the Spirit to teach you about God's Word, will, and ways by giving you wisdom and creative ideas for every area of your life, including how to steward your money, excel and prosper in your career, manage your time and schedule, prosper in relationships (in your home, church, office, ministry), function in ministry, and walk in purity and health (physically and emotionally).

Scripture

> The Holy Spirit...will teach you all things.
>
> —JOHN 14:26

Prayer

> *Holy Spirit, I ask You to lead me and teach me in every area of my life. Give me new ideas, order my steps, and open doors*

for new relationships and new business and ministry opportunities. Teach me how to live in a manner that is pleasing to You, and show me how best to walk in Your will, blessing, and prosperity for my life. Give me fresh insight into Your Word, Your will, Your ways, and Your heart.

Having an intimate relationship with the Holy Spirit will be of value to you in numerous ways. One of the most significant will be helping you to understand God's Word and incorporate it into your prayer life.

WHAT CAN I DO?

Come to the Lord from the starting place of profound thankfulness. With that as your foundation, you are positioned to "grow up" in wisdom and understanding.

FOR REFLECTION

"That . . . the Father of glory may give to you the spirit of wisdom and revelation in the knowledge of Him, the eyes of your understanding being enlightened" (Eph. 1:17–18).

Lord, like Moses, I declare, "Show me Your glory!" Teach me so that I am able to live in deep partnership with Your indwelling Holy Spirit.

How to Pray-Read the Word

*The power of prayer can never be overrated.... If
a man can but pray he can do anything. He
who knows how to overcome with God in
prayer has heaven and earth at his disposal.*

—CHARLES SPURGEON

TALKING TO GOD as we read the Word makes prayer easy and
enjoyable. We speak the truths of God's Word back to God as we
read. When I look back on forty years of walking with the Lord, I
realize that pray-reading the Word—using the Scripture as the "con-
versational material" for my communication with Jesus—*has been
the single most significant activity in my spiritual life*. This simple
activity is essential to abiding in Christ.

I vividly remember the day when John 5:39–40 hit me like a bolt
of lightning and radically shifted my understanding of prayer. I was
eighteen years old at the time and was just beginning my college
years. I had set aside time for daily prayer and Bible study, but as
I said earlier in this book, my prayer times were very boring. Then
I came across the passage in John that quotes Jesus as rebuking the
Pharisees for searching the Scriptures trying to find life in Bible
knowledge instead of in relationship with Him. They diligently
studied the Bible without connecting to God. They focused on the
written Word but neglected Jesus, the living Word. This passage
described me perfectly.

It suddenly became clear to me that I was seeking to find life
and experience the presence of God just by studying the Scripture
and gaining more Bible information. I came to understand that the

Scripture is like a "neon sign" pointing to Jesus. It testifies of Him. It tells us what His heart is like. Then I read verse 40: "You are not willing to come to Me so that you may have life." I instantly understood it to mean they did not talk to Him. Right then I got it—I needed to come to Jesus, to talk to Him, as I read the Bible. Coming to Jesus in this context speaks of more than having our sins forgiven. It is a call to commune with Him as we read the Bible.

In that moment I understood that as I read, I am to move from a purely "study mode" to a "dialogue mode" and talk to Jesus, the Word made flesh, through His written Word. I exclaimed, "Jesus, from now on I will talk to You when I read the Bible." The light went on that day, and I began my journey into what I term "pray-reading" the Word. I started that very hour, talking to Him over each phrase as I read the Word. I could feel His presence in a greater way, and I liked it. And it was amazing how things changed in my spiritual life! I began to love God's Word. This was a new feeling. I was filled with anticipation about where this practice might lead me.

It is now more than forty years later, and I have been on a glorious journey and adventure with Jesus and His Word all that time. I am not saying that it is glorious every time I read the Word. Some days when I pray-read the Bible it feels dull, but usually it is alive. This became my new way forward, and I stayed with it.

I believe you will have the same experience I did. Change will come, and you will begin to love reading the Word and praying. The change may not occur in a day; it will probably develop over time. But stay with it. I am certain you will be glad you did and that the effort will be worth it.

WHAT CAN I DO?

If you're a parent, think back to how enjoyable it was to read out loud to your children. Or maybe you can remember being read to this way as a child. Consider how much delight the Father takes in hearing you read His Word out loud to Him.

FOR REFLECTION

"You search the Scriptures, for in them you think you have eternal...life; and these are they which testify of Me. But you are not willing to *come to Me* [talk with Me] *that you may have life*" (John 5:39–40).

> *Lord, as I read Your Word today, allow me to see with new eyes and hear with new ears what You are saying. Help me to dialogue with You as You open the Scriptures to me in a fresh way.*

Appropriating God's Names

Shut the world out, withdraw from all worldly
thoughts and occupations, and shut yourself in
alone with God, to pray to Him in secret. Let
this be your chief object in prayer: to realize
the presence of your heavenly Father.

—ANDREW MURRAY

I WAS IMPACTED YEARS ago by Larry Lea's best-selling book *Could You Not Tarry One Hour?* in which he taught millions of people how to appropriate God's covenant names in prayer. I will share a few insights from his book because I believe appropriating God's names is a powerful way to grow in prayer.

Jesus taught us to pray that the Father's name be "hallowed" (Matt. 6:9). *To hallow* God's name means to sanctify, set apart, or praise it. In prayer we sanctify God's name by declaring it with a spirit of praise for the various truths implied by His name.

So how do we appropriate God's names? We declare them with faith and adoration in prayer. This activity results in the power and blessing associated with those truths being released in our lives.

When God gave Moses a special revelation of Himself, He used the name "YHWH," or as it is sometimes written, "Jehovah." This is God's covenant name, or the name He uses to emphasize His covenant with His people. This name was first given to Moses at the burning bush (Exod. 3:13–15), where God revealed Himself as the eternal God, who is self-existent, unchangeable, and transcendent. The Lord said, "I AM THAT I AM" (KJV). The Hebrew scribes considered this name too sacred to be spoken, so they used only four letters—"YHWH" or "JHVH"—to denote this unmentionable name of God, which is written in English as either "Yahweh" or "Jehovah."

In the Old Testament eight names of God are compounded with the covenant name "Jehovah" ("Yahweh"). All eight compound names reveal an aspect of the character of God and correspond to promises in the New Testament.

- Jehovah Tsidkenu: The Lord our righteousness
- Jehovah M'kaddesh: The Lord who sanctifies
- Jehovah Shammah: The Lord is there
- Jehovah Shalom: The Lord is peace
- Jehovah Rophe: The Lord heals
- Jehovah Jireh: The Lord's provision shall be seen
- Jehovah Nissi: The Lord my banner
- Jehovah Rohi: The Lord my shepherd

The Lord Jesus is our righteousness, sanctifier, peace, healer, provider, shepherd, banner, and the present One within us. These Old Testament names of God reveal different dimensions of His character that are expressed in Jesus.

WHAT CAN I DO?

Memorize each of God's covenant names so that you have them in your prayer arsenal whenever you need them. The Lord rejoices when He sees His sons and daughters declaring His majesty and splendor.

FOR REFLECTION

"This, then, is how you should pray: 'Our Father in heaven, hallowed be your name'" (Matt. 6:9).

Thank You, Jesus, for being the full embodiment of each one of these glorious attributes. I pray for deeper insight of each one! Lord, with faith and adoration, I declare that You are [specific covenant name] right now over my life. Thank You that even as I ask, You are already sending the answer.

_____

_____

_____

_____

_____

_____

_____

_____

_____

_____

_____

_____

_____

_____

_____

_____

_____

_____

_____

_____

Day 79

Prayer + Fasting

*Fasting helps express, deepen, confirm the resolution
that we are ready to sacrifice anything, even ourselves,
to attain what we seek for the kingdom of God.*

—ANDREW MURRAY

WHEN I FIRST came to know the Lord as a young man, I did not like fasting at all. Many times I would set my heart to spend the day in fasting and prayer, and within a few short hours, I was ready to quit, complaining, "Why did You set up Your kingdom this way? Why do You want me to sit here doing nothing except telling You what You already know and not eating? What is the point of this? Lord, I could be impacting many people if You would just let me do something instead of wasting my life away in prayer and fasting!" Nothing seemed more wasteful to me, but God was teaching me that His ways are higher and wiser than ours.

God has ordered His kingdom in such a way that some things that seem weak to men are actually powerful before God. In our natural minds we may argue against taking the time to pray and fast, but God wants us to understand that this is the way His power is most effectively released in our hearts and ministries.

There are several biblical principles related to fasting for you to be aware of as you begin to engage in this discipline. These principles describe fasting as an invitation, a paradox, a grace, and an expression of humility.

Fasting is an invitation—God does not require us to fast but rewards those who choose to fast: "When you fast...your Father who sees in secret will reward you openly" (Matt. 6:17–18). One

177

aspect of the Father's reward includes seeing more of His kingdom expressed in and through our lives and circumstances, as well as seeing our spiritual capacity enlarged to encounter more of His heart (which, of course, leads to experiencing more of His blessings). Fasting is for those who are hungry—hungry to experience more in their relationship with Jesus.

Fasting is a paradox—The paradox of fasting is that as we experience weakness in our flesh, we are strengthened in our spiritual lives; as we experience the pain of rawness, our hearts are tenderized before God and postured to receive more strength.

Fasting is a grace—We will not be able to sustain a lifestyle of fasting in our own strength; it is possible only by God's grace. I encourage you to ask for grace to enter into the mystery of connecting with God through fasting. We tell ourselves that fasting is too hard and that we will be too tired and uncomfortable, but in fact the fear of fasting is worse than the fasting itself. Our bodies were created to operate at their best with regular fasting. The practice of regular weekly fasting will help you develop a personal history in God in the grace of prayer and fasting.

Fasting is an expression of humility—David spoke of fasting as humbling himself before God (Ps. 35:13; 69:10). When we fast, our bodies are easily tired, our minds may not be clear, we feel unable to function at full capacity, and weakness seems to pervade everything we put our hands to. We find ourselves unable to do our work well. It humbles us to fast, and this is how God planned it. The Bible describes it as "humbling" or "afflicting" one's soul (Isa. 58:3, 5). Only desperate people—those who recognize their own great need and want to declare it to God—fast and pray.

WHAT CAN I DO?

Search out the different times in the Scripture where people fasted and see what God did. Then ask the Lord if He would give you grace to fast. What should you fast? Food? Social media? Sweets? Make the choice between just you and the Lord. Google "Daniel fast" and step out on a fast like Daniel did, eating mostly fruits, vegetables, and nuts, with set times of prayer each day.

FOR REFLECTION

"Blessed are those who hunger and thirst for righteousness, for they shall be filled" (Matt. 5:6).

Lord, as I set my heart to consecrate myself before You, strengthen me with grace to fast as part of my lifestyle. I humble myself before You, my God.

Seven Types of Biblical Fasting

*Prayer is the one hand with which we grasp
the invisible; fasting, the other, with which
we let loose and cast away the visible.*

—ANDREW MURRAY

WE FIND SEVEN types of fasting in Scripture. Please note that the categories overlap somewhat. Be sensitive to the Holy Spirit's leading to reveal which type of fast you may be called to in the coming days, weeks, or months.

1. Fasting to experience a greater measure of the power of God in personal ministry

We can fast for a greater release of God's power in our lives and ministries. Jesus referred to this type of fasting when the disciples could not set a demonized boy free (Matt. 17:21). The power of John the Baptist's preaching was undoubtedly connected to his fasted lifestyle (Matt. 11:18). The same can be said of the power in the apostle Paul's ministry. Fasting was a regular part of Paul's life.

Historians testify that the early church fasted twice a week (Wednesdays and Fridays) to experience more of God's power. Throughout church history many anointed men and women practiced regular fasting as they led great revivals.

2. Fasting for direction

Fasting positions us to receive more direction from the Lord. Throughout the New Testament we see that the early believers fasted for this purpose. Immediately after Paul's conversion on the road to Damascus, he fasted from food and drink for three days, waiting to receive clear direction from the Lord (Acts 9:9). A few years later Paul and the leaders of the church of Antioch fasted and prayed for direction. God spoke clearly, giving them a strategic mission assignment to reach the Gentiles by sending out Barnabas and Paul (Acts 13:1–2). Thus the first of Paul's missionary journeys was a direct result of corporate prayer, fasting, and seeking God, and it changed history.

3. Fasting for the fulfillment of God's promises

The Lord has plans and promises for each city on earth. The Lord intends for us to actively petition Him for their fulfillment. Scripture recounts many stories of men of faith whom God used to usher in the completion of His promises. Today, as we see multitudes headed for hell and the church struggling with spiritual barrenness, the biblical solution is clear. We must pray and fast until we see a breakthrough regarding the things God has promised our cities and nations.

4. Fasting to stop a crisis

Fasting to avert a national or individual crisis was a regular practice in Old Testament times. Over and over, God reversed Israel's desperate situation when they turned to Him in corporate prayer and fasting. Examples of humbling oneself with fasting during a time of personal crisis appear throughout Scripture as well. Hannah was so distressed by her physical barrenness that "she wept and did not eat" (1 Sam. 1:7) as she poured out her soul to God in prayer for a son. God answered her cry and lifted her barrenness by giving her a son who grew up to become the mighty prophet Samuel (1 Sam. 1:20).

5. Fasting for protection

The Scripture also gives examples of prayer with fasting for personal protection. Ezra the priest fasted and prayed, asking God for supernatural protection through foreign lands as he led a group of

Jews back to Jerusalem to help the Israelites already there rebuild the city.

After Haman set into motion a plan to annihilate all the Jews and take their possessions (Esther 3:13; 4:7), Queen Esther called the Jews in Persia to fast for three days, and they cried out in prayer with fasting (Esther 4:16). The Lord used her to reverse the situation among the Jews; thus He saved them from Haman's evil plan (Esther 9:1).

Church history is filled with examples of God's servants being delivered from peril and danger in response to prayer and fasting. The church today should be compelled to engage in these disciplines all the more as the days grow more evil. (See Luke 21:34–36.)

6. Fasting for insight into God's end-time plan

The Holy Spirit is raising up forerunner messengers who will have an increased measure of insight into what the Scripture says about Jesus' end-time plan. Daniel prophesied that in the end times, God would raise up people with prophetic understanding who would teach multitudes (Dan. 11:33–35; 12:4, 10). God answered Daniel's determination to gain prophetic insight into God's plans.

I believe the Lord will send angels to some of His end-time prophets as He did to Daniel to give increased insight into what is coming. Like Daniel, such people will have to set their hearts to gain more understanding through prayer and fasting.

7. Fasting for intimacy with God (the Bridegroom fast)

> The disciples of John came to Him, saying, "Why do we and the Pharisees fast often, but Your disciples do not fast?" And Jesus said to them, "Can the friends of the bridegroom mourn as long as the bridegroom is with them? But the days will come when the bridegroom will be taken away from them, and then they will fast."

—MATTHEW 9:14–15

In these verses Jesus spoke of a new kind of fast based on His identity as the Bridegroom God and the disciples' desire to be with Him. It is a fast motivated primarily by one's desire for Jesus rather than by a need for more power, direction in ministry, divine intervention or protection, and so on.

We were made to love and be loved by God, and He has made us to crave Him until our hearts' cries are answered. He increases our experience of Him through the process of both awakening and answering desires within us.

WHAT CAN I DO?

Reread the seven types of fasting. See which one resonates with you then schedule a time to fast according to that pattern in the next two weeks.

FOR REFLECTION

"Are they ministers of Christ?...I [Paul] am more...in fastings often" (2 Cor. 11:23, 27).

Lord, make me sensitive to the leading of Your Holy Spirit so that I will know when I am called to fast, and the intention of Your heart in calling the fast.

_____

_____

_____

_____

_____

_____

Day 81

Praying in the Spirit

If the spiritual life be healthy, under the full power of
the Spirit, praying without ceasing will be natural.

—ANDREW MURRAY

IN HIS FIRST letter to the Corinthians, Paul described two different types of the gift of tongues—two different expressions, with two different purposes. I had missed this key point in my early ministry when I taught that the gift of tongues was not available to every believer.

Once I saw that there were two different types of tongues in the Bible, I understood that two seemingly contradictory views of tongues are both biblical: (1) that only *some* believers, not *all*, have the gift of tongues (1 Cor. 12:30); and (2) that "all" can receive the gift of tongues (1 Cor. 14:5; Mark 16:17). I also came to see that there is a significant difference between the gift of tongues given for the *profit of the corporate body* (1 Cor. 12:7), when the speaker speaks to men, and tongues given as a devotional prayer language for the *profit of the individual* who uses the gift to speak privately to God (1 Cor. 14:2, 4).

Paul distinguished between the public and private use of the gift of tongues. In 1 Corinthians 14:18–19 he thanked God that he spoke in tongues more than others but said that when he was in church, he would rather speak five words with his understanding than 10,000 words in tongues. In other words, his "speaking in tongues more than anyone" referred to using his personal prayer language, not to giving utterance in tongues in a public church service. Here he makes a clear distinction between the two types of speaking in tongues.

Jesus said that speaking in new tongues was one of the signs that would follow those who believe (Mark 16:17). Therefore, every believer can receive the gift of tongues for his *personal use* as a devotional prayer language, but not all will receive the gift of tongues for *public use* in a church service.

WHAT CAN I DO?

Be careful not to neglect your personal prayer language (tongues). Use it in your prayer closet and when you are gathered with other believers during a time of corporate prayer (softly).

FOR REFLECTION

"I thank my God I speak with tongues more than you all; yet in the church I would rather speak five words with my understanding, that I may teach others also, than ten thousand words in a tongue" (1 Cor. 14:18–19).

> *Father, thank You for the gift of the Holy Spirit—my devotional prayer language. Stir up the gift within me so that I can truly pray without ceasing.*

Day 82

Benefits of Speaking in Tongues

Men may reject our message, oppose our arguments
or despise us, but they are helpless against our prayers.

—Sidlow Baxter

I N 1 Corinthians 14 Paul gave three benefits of speaking in
tongues: speaking mysteries (v. 2); edifying oneself (v. 4); and
blessing and giving thanks to God (v. 17).

Speaking mysteries

> For he who speaks in a tongue does not speak to men but
> to God, for no one understands him; however, in the spirit
> he speaks mysteries.
>
> —1 Corinthians 14:2

When we speak in tongues, we commune with the Holy Spirit,
who sometimes gives us information that helps us to understand
God's will and heart for us. Speaking mysteries is not about receiving
"special truths" that are available to only a few. As we speak mysteries
in tongues—in our prayer language—we may receive faint and subtle
impressions from the Lord in the same way that words of knowledge
come to us. These impressions may give us insight into how God
wants to touch us or someone else through our prayers.

The Holy Spirit possesses full knowledge of the Father and the
Son—one preacher spoke of Him as the ultimate "search engine" of
God's heart. He is the only one who knows the deep things of the
Father and the Son. He gives us a portion of what He searches out as
we engage more with Him by speaking to Him with our minds and
by praying with our spirits.

186

Edifying oneself

> He who speaks in a tongue *edifies himself,* but he who
> prophesies edifies the church.
>
> —1 CORINTHIANS 14:4

Paul was calling us not to be self-centered but to build up our
spiritual lives. He was essentially encouraging us to "charge our spiritual batteries." Edifying oneself simply means being strengthened or
built up. Jude 20 also speaks of "praying in the Holy Spirit" to build
up our personal faith. Doing so results in our hearts becoming more
tender and sensitive to the things of the Holy Spirit and enables us
to receive mysteries and give thanks to God (1 Cor. 14:16). Being edified in our spiritual lives is an essential aspect of walking in the Spirit
and ministering in His power. I have never known anyone who oper-
ated in the prophetic or the healing ministry who did not speak in
tongues regularly in his private prayer time.

Paul referred several times to the idea of praying night and day
or praying without ceasing (1 Thess. 3:10; 5:17). I'm sure that one
way he was able to pray so consistently was by praying in tongues
while doing other things, such as making tents (Acts 18:3; 20:34)
or walking from one city to the next. When his hands were sewing
tents, his heart was engaged in God as he prayed much in the Spirit.
As I came to understand that praying in tongues is helpful in edifying our spiritual lives and growing in the things of the Spirit, I was
provoked to seek to pray without ceasing by praying in tongues at
least part of the time.

Blessing and thanking God

> If you bless with the spirit, how will he who occupies
> the place of the uninformed say "Amen" at your giving of
> thanks...? For you indeed give thanks well.
>
> —1 CORINTHIANS 14:16–17

When we pray in the Spirit, we are actually ministering to God by blessing and giving thanks to Him, and He receives our thanks. Thus, speaking in tongues is a devotional gift that we use to bless, praise, and worship God in a way that differs from giving thanks only with our minds.

When I pray in tongues, I often focus my mind on the scene centered on God's throne in heaven (see Revelation 23:4) and talk directly to the Father. At other times I speak to the Holy Spirit, who dwells in my spirit (Rom. 8:9; 2 Cor. 13:14). I encourage people to talk to the indwelling Spirit. Eastern religions look inwardly but to nothingness. This is a great error. We look to a real person, the indwelling Holy Spirit.

WHAT CAN I DO?

Notice how stirred up and edified you are when you speak in tongues. Trust that the Holy Spirit is speaking mysteries through you, and let Him have His way.

FOR REFLECTION

"The Spirit searches all things, yes, the deep things of God…we have received…the Spirit who is from God, that we might know the things that have been freely given to us by God" (1 Cor. 2:10, 12).

> *Lord, thank You for the gift of tongues, which edifies and builds up my spirit.*

_____

_____

_____

_____

_____

Day 83

Singing in the Spirit

*Surely that which occupies the total time
and energies of heaven [worship and prayer]
must be a fitting pattern for earth.*

—Paul E. Billheimer

God designed the human makeup so that our spirits could engage with God by speaking or *singing* in tongues (1 Cor. 14:15; Eph. 5:19; Col. 3:16). Both singing with our spirit and singing with our understanding are important in our spiritual lives. Paul taught that if we sing the Scripture from our hearts, we will experience God's grace and the Spirit's presence. (See Ephesians 5:18–19.)

Our hearts are warmed and tenderized by spontaneously singing the Word and singing with our spirit; doing so makes us more sensitive to the Holy Spirit. I have discovered the power of spontaneously singing Bible passages to God and intermittently singing in tongues, which often results in the Holy Spirit's touching the deep chambers of my heart. I encourage you to do this regularly.

Singing the Word impacts our hearts more than just speaking it or hearing others speak it. God designed the human heart to be touched deeply by music and singing. As we sing the Word and sing with our spirit, we receive mysteries (divine impressions from the Holy Spirit) and gain insight from the Word. The Holy Spirit will give us more and more if we will sing the Word and sing with our spirit consistently.

Clearly our communion with God is strengthened through praying or singing in tongues because our spirits are engaged with God in a way that extends beyond praying with our minds. Praying or singing in tongues enables us to speak and receive mysteries (1 Cor. 14:2), to edify ourselves (v. 4), to bless God (v. 16), and to pray continually (v. 18) in a way that builds up our faith. Thus it tenderizes our hearts and sensitizes us to the things of the Holy Spirit.

The good news is that any believer can pray in the Spirit because it requires no special training or intellectual ability. It is a spiritual gift that can benefit us greatly as we grow in prayer. Employing this gift makes it easier to sustain prayer for long periods because we do not have to keep finding different ways of expressing our ideas. Our spirits commune effortlessly with the Holy Spirit when we pray in tongues.

WHAT CAN I DO?

As you go about your day, be intentional about praying in the Spirit. I urge you to make this a part of your daily communion with the Lord. In your car or as you go for a walk, engage in speaking or singing in the Spirit.

FOR REFLECTION

"Let the word of Christ dwell in you richly in all wisdom, teaching and admonishing one another in psalms and hymns and spiritual songs, singing with grace in your hearts to the Lord" (Col. 3:16).

Lord, I want to sing praises to Your name both with my understanding and in the Spirit.

Day 84

Receiving the Gift of Tongues

*There is a general kind of praying which fails
for lack of precision. It is as if a regiment of
soldiers should all fire off their guns anywhere.
Possibly somebody would be killed, but the
majority of the enemy would be missed.*

—CHARLES SPURGEON

EVERY PERSON WHO has received Jesus and His free gift of salvation has access to the gift of tongues as a personal prayer language. If you have never received your devotional prayer language (the gift of tongues), then you can ask for it now. It is very simple: just ask the Father to release this particular grace of the Spirit to you.

Some say if the Spirit wants them to speak in tongues, then He will make them. However, the Spirit will not "force" anyone to do anything, including speaking in tongues. Some wait for an overwhelming sense of the Spirit, but often the Spirit touches His people like a gentle breeze. Therefore, as you pray for the gift of tongues, you may feel the presence of God lightly, or you may feel a gentle urge to speak out. I encourage you to speak out the words the Spirit gives you in your new prayer language and see what happens. It is not always powerful—sometimes it begins very gently and subtly. God is faithful to give good gifts to His children when they ask Him. If you desire to grow in prayer, I encourage you to use this gift regularly.

Paul told the Corinthians, "Do not forbid to speak with tongues" (1 Cor. 14:39). To forbid ourselves from speaking in tongues is to minimize the blessing of edifying ourselves spiritually and of speaking mysteries, thus diminishing our ability to experience the things of the Spirit. I know of no one who operates in the prophetic ministry or healing who does not speak in tongues.

Praying in tongues is a universal benefit for all believers. It is not a requirement or proof of salvation; rather, it is a benefit available to us through the work of Jesus and the indwelling of the Spirit. It is not reserved for those with a special calling. It does not require any special training, qualification, or preparation. It is a free gift to all because of the blood of Jesus. It is a free gift to all as a part of the benefits of our salvation.

WHAT CAN I DO?

If you've never received the gift of tongues, ask the Father in your quiet time today and open your mouth to praise Him in a new tongue. It's OK if only a few syllables come out. As you practice, you'll become more fluent and notice a new language emerging.

FOR REFLECTION

"Therefore, brethren, desire earnestly to prophesy, and do not forbid to speak with tongues" (1 Cor. 14:39).

> *Lord, thank You for the gift of praying in tongues. You are a good Father who gives good gifts to His children.*

Day 85

Receiving the Spirit of Prayer

*Prayer is both starting point and goal to
every movement in which are the elements of
permanent progress. Wherever the church is
aroused...somebody, somewhere has been praying.*

—A. T. PIERSON

JUST AS JESUS is an intercessor, so the Holy Spirit is also an intercessor. He intercedes for God's will to be done on earth. He prays
both *for* us and *through* us. At times He pours out on intercessors a
spirit of supplication that is commonly referred to as "the spirit of
prayer." The spirit of prayer is a special grace given by the Spirit that
empowers prayer in and through the body of Christ.

The spirit of prayer, or the gift of anointed prayer, is manifest
through us in special moments when we are touched with an unusual
measure of the Spirit's activity that goes beyond the normal measure of grace we commonly experience in prayer. It is a great blessing
when a spirit of prayer rests on us. Our hearts are especially tenderized as the presence of the Spirit rests on us to anoint and energize
us in our prayers. These are powerful times of participation with the
Holy Spirit in prayer.

Paul tells us that at times the Spirit prays through us with sighs
and groans too deep to articulate with words. He gives impetus to
a prayer burden being expressed through us in a form of travail that
releases a greater measure of God's power. Through my studies of
others and my own personal experience, I have come to understand
that the groans that are characteristic of this form of travail have no
words and are often accompanied by gentle weeping.

Some assume that when the Spirit is tenderly or deeply moving on their hearts, they should stir themselves up by saying more. It is better to go in the opposite direction—to quiet our hearts and pay attention to the Holy Spirit's leadership.

My experiences have taught me that the burden of the Spirit will be sustained longer and go deeper if we give ourselves to the groaning and tender weeping by "going inward"—focusing on the indwelling Spirit—instead of "going outward" and articulating our prayers in English in a fast and loud way. I have learned through experience that travail is generally more quiet than loud because we are interacting deeply with the indwelling Spirit.

Travailing prayer may be as short as fifteen minutes, or it may last much longer. I have occasionally experienced groaning in the Spirit that lasted for hours. It is not something we can imitate, initiate, or stir up by our own zeal. Travail is a sovereign work of the Holy Spirit, as is every manifestation of the spirit of prayer.

WHAT CAN I DO?

Allow the Spirit to take you "inward" for deep, travailing prayer when the need arises. Resist the temptation to help the Spirit out. See how He guides your time of travailing in the Spirit.

FOR REFLECTION

"In the same way the Spirit also helps our weakness; for we do not know how to pray as we should, but the Spirit Himself intercedes for us with groanings too deep for words" (Rom. 8:26, NASB).

> *Lord, grow me to the point where I am sensitive to Your Holy Spirit. When You are burdened, I want to feel some of the burdens that You feel and engage my heart with Yours.*

_____

_____

_____

_____

_____

_____

_____

_____

_____

_____

_____

_____

_____

_____

_____

_____

_____

_____

_____

_____

_____

_____

_____

_____

_____

Day 86

Three Modes of Prayer

The man who mobilizes the Christian church
to pray will make the greatest contribution.

Andrew Murray

How glorious and powerful it is when the Holy Spirit releases a spirit of prayer on and through us! It is worth setting everything aside to follow His leadership during these special times of prayer. Unfortunately, not all our prayer times are infused with the spirit of prayer. Praying under its influence is only one of three different modes of prayer that I have identified. I use the analogy of an ancient warship, powered by rows of oarsmen and sails, to describe these three modes.

The first mode of prayer is like the warship on a *calm day,* with only a gentle breeze. The gentle breeze helps a little, but in order to make good progress, the oarsmen have to row hard. This mode represents our normal daily prayer times. We put effort into it, as the oarsmen do. We advance, and we are grateful for the small breeze, but it takes more effort on our parts to continue in prayer in order to make progress.

The second mode of prayer is like the warship on a windy day. The ship's sails catch a strong wind while the oarsmen are rowing. All of a sudden the ship is carried along at a high speed without much human effort. It may go ten times faster. This mode represents our prayer times under the spirit of prayer. We may start out rowing, but suddenly the wind of the Spirit carries us along so that we make far greater progress that day.

The third mode of prayer is like the warship facing into a heavy wind. The oarsmen are rowing as hard as they can, but the ship is being blown backward instead of forward. This mode represents the prayer times in which we experience heightened demonic resistance. In these times the strong resisting winds of darkness may hit our minds and hearts and make us feel as if we are losing ground, no matter how hard we row. In reality we are not losing ground because it is impossible to pray in God's will and lose ground in prayer.

In times of heightened demonic opposition, we must persevere with confidence, knowing that God hears our prayers offered in the name of Jesus and that His authority makes our breakthrough certain. (See 1 John 5:14.) Satan must always flee when we stand with confidence using the name of Jesus against him.

I have found that most of my normal, everyday prayer life takes place in the first prayer mode, comparable to the warship on a calm day, when it is necessary for the oarsmen to exert effort in their rowing to make any headway. However, when I least expect it, the "winds" of the Holy Spirit suddenly help me in my weakness. It is a glorious thing for the Holy Spirit to tenderize our hearts as He anoints and energizes our prayers, allowing us to participate with Him in fulfilling God's plans and purposes on the earth.

WHAT CAN I DO?

Be sensitive to the Holy Spirit, and like a good sailor, watch for the changing winds as needed. If your heart continues to be engaged with the Lord you will develop spiritual discernment.

FOR REFLECTION

"Now this is the confidence that we have in Him, that if we ask anything according to His will, He hears us" (1 John 5:14).

Lord, whether I am facing calm days, windy days, or storm-tossed days, I am grateful that I have a constant lifeline to You through prayer.

Day 87

The Throne of God

Before a word of petition is offered, we should have
the definite consciousness that we are talking to
God, and should believe that He is listening and
is going to grant the thing that we ask of Him.

—R. A. TORREY

ALTHOUGH WE MAY not often think of it in this way, when we pray we actually come before God's throne—a real throne, with a real person sitting on it. Hebrews 4:16 says, "Let us then approach God's throne of grace with confidence, so that we may receive mercy and find grace to help us in our time of need" (NIV). What an amazing privilege, that mere mortals can approach the throne of the eternal One, who rules the universe and waits for us to ask for help!

We are strengthened in our prayer lives by learning about the One to whom we pray, and that includes the place where He dwells and the majestic scene that surrounds Him—because it reveals His beauty in a unique way. When we understand the kind of God He is, our relationship with Him deepens, our minds are renewed by the truth, and the way that we pray changes: prayer becomes more enjoyable and thus sustainable.

When I pray, rather than speaking my words into the air or praying in a mental vacuum, I focus my mind on the biblical description of God's throne as set forth by the apostle John in Revelation 4.

> Behold, a throne set in heaven, and One sat on the throne. And He who sat there was like a jasper and a sardius stone in appearance; and there was a rainbow around the throne...like an emerald. Around the throne were

twenty-four thrones, and on the thrones I saw twenty-four elders sitting, clothed in white robes; and they had crowns of gold on their heads. And from the throne proceeded lightnings, thunderings, and voices. Seven lamps of fire were burning before the throne, which are the seven Spirits of God. Before the throne there was a sea of glass, like crystal. And...around the throne, were four living creatures...they do not rest day or night, saying: "Holy, holy, holy, Lord God Almighty, who was and is and is to come!"

—REVELATION 4:2–6, 8

This is the clearest and most detailed depiction of God's throne in the Bible. Scenes like this in the Scriptures are a great gift to the body of Christ because they show us what God wanted us to understand about His beautiful, majestic throne. Over the next several days, we will explore the scene around the Father's throne, the place where He receives our prayers.

Having a mental picture of what is happening around the throne can be an incredible reminder that the Father and the Son are listening to us from their royal court—the governmental center of the universe and the ultimate place of beauty.

WHAT CAN I DO?

Read Revelation 4 and picture the scene around God's throne. Envision God on His throne with Jesus the Son on His throne beside Him, both inclining their ears to hear your prayers.

FOR REFLECTION

"Let us then approach God's throne of grace with confidence, so that we may receive mercy and find grace to help us in our time of need" (Heb. 4:16, NIV).

Lord, I come confidently before Your throne. Help me to always realize that I am not just speaking into the air. I'm talking with a real person who loves to hear my prayers.

Day 88

Beholding the Beauty of God

Prayer is the soul's traffic with Heaven;
God comes down to us by His Spirit,
and we go up to Him by prayer.

—THOMAS WATSON

DAVID'S LIFELONG GOAL, from his youth to his elderly years, was to regularly encounter the beauty of God. This should be the aim of our lives as well—to engage in the realm of God's beauty for our entire lives. And there is no better place to understand the beauty of the Lord than the epicenter of all beauty—the throne of God.

When speaking about the generation when the Lord returns, the prophet Isaiah declared, "Your eyes will see the King in His beauty" (Isa. 33:17). The King is Jesus, and the implication of Isaiah's prophecy is that His beauty would be a particular emphasis of the Holy Spirit in the generation of the Lord's return.

It is significant that right after the throne scene in chapters 4 and 5, the Book of Revelation goes on to describe the intense pressure and persecution of the end-time generation. The whole narrative of the Book of Revelation is rooted in the revelation of the beauty of the throne. In this, God is preparing His church for the unique dynamics that are unfolding in the Book of Revelation. We're going to need to see the King in His beauty in a more dynamic way in order to thrive spiritually amid the negative and positive of the end-time generation.

My prayer for IHOP-KC and the body of Christ is Psalm 45, where the psalmist said his heart was overflowing with a good theme—the beauty of the King. Though we might lose sight of it here and there, may we constantly realign our hearts to overflow with the reality of God's beauty.

WHAT CAN I DO?

To *behold* is to see or perceive. As we behold God's beauty, our eyes are opened to a deeper reality of who God is in our lives and in the earth. Ask God to give you a deeper understanding of who He is and cause others to see His beauty in you as you go about your day.

FOR REFLECTION

"One thing I have desired of the Lord, that will I seek: that I may dwell in the house of the Lord all the days of my life, to behold the beauty of the Lord, and to inquire in His temple" (Ps. 27:4).

> *Lord, open the eyes of my heart so I behold Your beauty. I want to remain confident in You even when troubles intensify in my life. May I never doubt Your goodness and love for me.*

Day 89

God Is Light

I know, whenever I have prayed earnestly,
that I have been amply heard, and have
obtained more than I prayed for. God indeed
sometimes delayed, but at last He came.

—MARTIN LUTHER

IN THE REVELATION 4 picture of the throne of God, we see the beauty of God's person—how God looks. In verse 3, John said that He who sat on the throne "was like a jasper and a sardius stone in appearance; and there was a rainbow around the throne, in appearance like an emerald." John gives us only hints at God's appearance, but we see from this verse that color radiates out of God's being.

Jasper is like the brightness of diamonds. Can you imagine? This crystal-like brightness just emanates out of God's being. The brightness doesn't just surround Him; it emanates out of Him because He *is* light. First Timothy 6:16 says God dwells in unapproachable light, and the reason God's light is unapproachable is not because God wants to create distance from us.

This bright, unapproachable light is actually a protection because in our humanity, we don't have the capacity to handle the intensity of God's raw presence. Only when we have our resurrected bodies will we be able to come close to that powerful light. And yet even the angels stand at a distance. Those that are nearest Him, the seraphim, cover their eyes, and when they get a glimpse of Him, they cover their eyes again before they come up for air to get another glimpse. This goes on and on through the eternal ages. Those nearest to His throne never tire of seeing His beauty.

This is where we come when we go to God in prayer. This is who we have access to; when we're before the throne speaking into the Father's heart, this is the One we're talking to, singing to, and worshipping— the One who is clothed in light, the One whose brightness leaves celestial beings in awe. We cannot in our flesh behold such glory, but this great God inclines His ear to hear our prayers. Again and again, God covers the distance between Himself and His children, giving us access to all He is—His beautiful, fascinating, and terrifying glory.

WHAT CAN I DO?

As you begin your prayer time, take a minute to align your mind with the scene around the throne. Behold God's beauty and the light emanating from His presence. Allow your awareness of His glory to embolden you in prayer.

FOR REFLECTION

"I will meditate on the glorious splendor of Your majesty, and on Your wondrous works" (Ps. 145:5).

> *Lord, You are robed in light too wonderful for my eyes to behold. Yet You incline Your ear to hear my prayers (Ps. 116:2). Thank You for the wondrous works You have done and continue to do in my life.*

Day 90

The Fiery Passion of God

Effective prayer is prayer that attains what it seeks.
It is prayer that moves God, effecting its end.

—Charles G. Finney

GOD IS BEAUTIFUL in His appearance, not just His character. The throne of God is the epicenter and perfection of all beauty. In Revelation 4, John said God's appearance is like a sardius stone, which is a deep-red gem.

John saw a fiery, ruby red brightness emanating out of God's being. Moses saw this and described God as a consuming fire. The sardius reflects the fiery passion of God's heart. Our God is a consuming fire. He is a jealous God. This is not a sinful, human jealousy. It's not a jealousy born out of weakness or lack. This jealousy is selfless, intense, pure love.

The fiery red emanating out of His being represents not only what God looks like but also what His heart looks like and what He feels. God is jealous—He is intensely engaged with His people. He's not disconnected from what's happening in the affairs of the earth or your life. The sardius radiance emanating out of Him is expressing the deep desire of His heart. At the very core of God's personality is a consuming love for His people. As you come into His presence, envision the deep red of the sardius and remember that this is how intensely the Father loves you.

WHAT CAN I DO?

Actively remind yourself of the Father's love for you. Make a list of scriptures that speak of God's beauty and His love for you.

206

Determine to speak those truths regularly back to God with gratitude and affection.

FOR REFLECTION

"For the Lord your God is a consuming fire, a jealous God" (Deut. 4:24).

> *Lord, I marvel at Your great love for me. You pay attention to everything that happens to me and are concerned about every issue I face. I choose to cast all my cares upon You because I know You care for me.*

The Mercy of God

*Storm the throne of grace and persevere
therein, and mercy will come down.*

—JOHN WESLEY

AT THE THRONE of God, John tells us "there was a rainbow...in appearance like an emerald" (Rev. 4:3). This rainbow reveals how God acts.

You may recall in Genesis 9 that God set a rainbow in the clouds as a sign of His promise to never again destroy the earth by flood. The rainbow that appeared in the sky was a reflection of the rainbow that has appeared around the throne from eternity past. And it's a declaration of God's mercy.

Psalm 145:9 says everything that God does, He does in tender mercy. Although God has total power, He expresses it with tender mercy. Even His judgments are tender mercy, because He is confronting the things that hinder love to move those obstacles out of the way.

What a remarkable reality. At the throne of God, His glorious power, His fiery love, and His tender mercy are all brought together. The fierceness of the Lion and the tenderness of the Lamb are manifested at the Father's throne. This picture is a true reflection of the Father's heart. Can't you see that we have it made? This is the God we're talking to when we pray!

WHAT CAN I DO?

Sometimes we avoid prayer when we feel we've messed up because we think God is angry with us. When you miss the mark, picture the emerald rainbow emanating from God's throne. Let it remind you of God's tender mercy and cause you to run to His throne in prayer.

FOR REFLECTION

"But God, who is rich in mercy, because of His great love with which He loved us, even when we were dead in trespasses, made us alive together with Christ (by grace you have been saved), and raised us up together, and made us sit together in the heavenly places in Christ Jesus, that in the ages to come He might show the exceeding riches of His grace in His kindness toward us in Christ Jesus" (Eph. 2:4–7).

Lord, because of Your great mercy, I have access to Your glorious throne. And although You are all-powerful, anger doesn't emanate from You. Rather, I see Your passionate love and Your tender mercy at Your throne. I choose to come to You boldly, even when I've failed, because You abound in mercy.

The Beauty of God's People

*There is no way that Christians, in a private capacity,
can do so much to promote the work of God and
advance the kingdom of Christ as by prayer.*

—Jonathan Edwards

God's beauty is also manifested in His people, and is seen in the exaltation of the saints as they are enthroned, robed, and crowned. In Revelation 4:4, John wrote that "around the throne were twenty-four thrones, and on the thrones I saw twenty-four elders sitting, clothed in white robes; they had crowns of gold on their heads." Some say these elders are angels, but most Bible commentators see them as people who have been redeemed.

In this we see the dignity and value of the redeemed. God so cleanses, forgives, equips, and exalts His former enemies that now they are on thrones reigning with Him. This is almost inconceivable. God includes broken human beings in the inner circle of His government forever. The angels are glorious, but they are not in the government; they are the servants of the redeemed!

Eye has not seen; ear has not heard; it's never entered into your mind or my mind the fullness of who we are in Christ. We hardly have a clue. We can't even imagine the glory of who we are. The devil tells you that you're worthless, you're a failure, your life is meaningless. But he is a liar! Your life has indescribable value.

God puts His former enemy in the top places of government. What kind of king would do that? Historically, when kings captured their enemies, they exiled them or put them away somewhere because they were a threat to their power. But God redeemed His enemies and said, "I'm going to put them on thrones." The world exploits the weak, but God exalts the weak. There's no one like our God. There's absolutely no one like Him!

WHAT CAN I DO?

As you pray, consider how God sees you—cleansed, forgiven, redeemed, and ruling and reigning with Christ. Visualize the elders around the throne and remind yourself that you pray from a position of authority and security through Christ.

FOR REFLECTION

"Eye has not seen...the things which God has prepared for those who love Him" (1 Cor. 2:9).

> *Lord, thank You for partnering with Your people to accomplish Your will. I know You have an incredible purpose for my life, and I choose to partner with You in prayer to see Your plans prevail in the earth.*

Day 93

Robed in Righteousness

*No one's a firmer believer in the power
of prayer than the devil; not that he
practices it, but he suffers from it.*

—GUY H. KING

THE TWENTY-FOUR ELDERS that John saw around God's throne were "clothed in white robes; and they had crowns of gold on their heads" (Rev. 4:4). Jewish readers would have immediately associated these robes with the priesthood, as that was one of the main characteristics of the priest.

This verse speaks of the priestly ministry of the saints. Although we have this ministry in fullness in the age to come, we also have this ministry now. God has redeemed His people, and we reveal God to the created order even now. We reveal God to others. We release His power and purposes in the earth. God could wave His hand like He did in Genesis 1 and cause His will to manifest, but He chooses to work through people. And one way He works through us is through prayer.

The same verse in Revelation 4 says the elders are crowned. This speaks of eternal rewards. God remembers and rewards the multitude of large and small acts of love and obedience you perform in your lifetime. In the span of seventy years, you might manage a couple of big acts of obedience, but almost all of our acts of obedience are very, very small. Yet God notices each one. He remembers every cup of cold water you gave someone who was thirsty, every need you helped meet in big and small ways. God remembers and rewards everything.

The crowns the elders are wearing are victor's crowns, like the kind one receives after running a race. But as Christians we are not racing against one another. We're racing to push against the powers of darkness that are resisting us so we can enter into our fullness. Beloved, this is your story—to be enthroned, robed, and clothed forever.

WHAT CAN I DO?

We think of receiving rewards for the big acts of obedience, but God honors even the small things—including giving someone a cup of cold water (Matt. 10:42). Ask God to show you how you can reveal His goodness to someone today and honor Him in even the smallest of ways.

FOR REFLECTION

"Finally, there is laid up for me the crown of righteousness, which the Lord, the righteous Judge, will give to me on that Day, and not to me only but also to all who have loved His appearing" (2 Tim. 4:8).

Father, I get excited just thinking about what awaits me as Your child. May I always honor You, even in the small things. Like the twenty-four elders, I fall down before You in lovesick adoration. You are worthy of all my praise.

Day 94

The Beauty of God's Power

*Perhaps you will have to spend hours on your knees
or upon your face before the throne. Never mind.
Wait. God will do great things for you if you will
wait for Him. Yield to Him. Cooperate with Him.*

—JOHN SMITH

IN REVELATION 4:5, John described lightnings, thunderings, and voices proceeding from God's throne. This is just my theory, but I see the lightning as a visual demonstration of God's power being manifest to the earth. I believe that in heaven, whenever this energy of God is released to touch the natural world, there is a visual dimension of it around the throne in the form of lightning. So I think the lightning is more than just a beautiful display; I think it is an indicator of what the Father is doing by the Spirit.

Habakkuk 3:4 says that when the Messiah, Jesus, returns, lightning will come out of His hands. I believe the same power manifested during Jesus' earthly ministry, but nobody could see the lightning; they saw the body get healed or the demonized person delivered. However, in the age to come they will see the demonstration of God's power, and they will see the lightning! God has an abundance of power, and He loves the beauty and glory of lightning breaking out of His throne.

Not only is there lightning, there is also thunder. Thunder is mentioned frequently in the Bible, and often it is associated with a particular message God is declaring. So I believe the thunder represents God saying, "I am a God who communicates. I will speak to you and through you, and it will resound in your being like thunder."

God is not going to remain veiled. He is not disinterested. Our God will share His secrets openly. (See Psalm 25.)

Finally, there are voices around God's throne—various sounds, songs, and music (Rev. 4:5; 8:5; 11:19; 16:18). I believe the sounds emanating from God's throne will be majestic, gloriously terrifying sounds that are full of power. And then there is music and singing. God is described in Zephaniah 3:17 as singing over His people. David was the great psalmist of Israel, but he is only a picture of the ultimate singer over Israel. Jesus is the greatest singer, musician, and songwriter who has ever walked on the earth. And the songs that are being released throughout heaven are going to fill the earth.

We are going to be living in this realm of beauty, but it is not only for a time to come; we have glimpses of it even now. As we meditate on these themes, may they inspire and energize us to love God. That is what this beauty dimension of God does for us.

WHAT CAN I DO?

Begin your prayer time by envisioning the lightnings, thunderings, and voices around the throne. Ask God to reveal Himself to you in a dynamic way today.

FOR REFLECTION

"His coming is as brilliant as the sunrise. Rays of light flash from his hands, where his awesome power is hidden" (Hab. 3:4, NLT).

> *Lord, Your power emanates from Your throne. May it also be manifest in my life today and always.*

215

Day 95

The Beauty of God's Presence

*To the man who prays habitually (not only
when he feels like it—that is one of the snares
of religion—but also when he does not feel
like it) Christ is sure to make Himself real.*

—James Stewart

God's beauty is seen in how the Spirit imparts His presence to strengthen His people. Looking again at Revelation 4, we see:

> Seven lamps of fire were burning before the throne, which are the seven Spirits of God. Before the throne there was a sea of glass, like crystal.... And around the throne, were four living creatures.

> —Revelation 4:5–6

Here we see a depiction of the Holy Spirit's ministry. John was careful to say in verse 5 that the seven lamps of fire were not ordinary lamps but represented the Holy Spirit. These seven "Spirits of God" are the diverse, glorious manifestations of the presence of the Holy Spirit (Isa. 11:2; Rev. 1:4; 3:1; 5:6).

In front of the throne there is a sea of glass, like crystal. Later, in Revelation 15:2, we read that the saints will gather on a sea of glass-like crystal in God's fire: "And I saw something like a sea of glass mingled with fire, and those who have the victory over the beast, over his image and over his mark and over the number of his name, standing on the sea of glass, having harps of God."

When I read this verse, I picture us on the sea of glass, perhaps billions of saints standing there before God's throne, worshipping

Him. And the seven lamps of fire represent the fire of God—the Holy Spirit—on the sea in the midst of the worship.

I don't think of the lamps as little table lamps. I picture them like the pillar of fire that appeared at night when the Israelites were in the wilderness. I don't believe that pillar was a small flicker but something so large it terrified the heathen nations around them when they saw it. The seven lamps of fire undoubtedly will be far more magnificent in size and in splendor than the pillar of fire that accompanied the Israelites, because they will be manifestations of the Holy Spirit as He moves over the sea of saints in the midst of their worship.

The Upper Room on the day of Pentecost is just a snapshot of the great worship gathering taking place around the throne. And that is what we approach when we go before God in prayer.

WHAT CAN I DO?

Read Psalm 103 as a prayer. Invite the Holy Spirit to dwell in the midst of your worship.

FOR REFLECTION

"Then there appeared to them divided tongues, as of fire, and one sat upon each of them. And they were all filled with the Holy Spirit and began to speak with other tongues, as the Spirit gave them utterance" (Acts 2:3–4).

> *Lord, I ask You for a fresh impartation of Your Spirit. I ask for a taste of what we will experience around Your throne.*

Day 96

The Burning Ones

Where there is much prayer, there will be much of the Spirit; where there is much of the Spirit, there will be ever-increasing prayer.

—Andrew Murray

AROUND THE THRONE were four living creatures like a lion, a calf, a man, and an eagle. These four living creatures are *seraphim*, which means "the burning ones." Although the four living creatures really look the way they are described, I believe they also are prophetic statements of how the redeemed will relate to and serve God. They are a reminder to us of our purpose as believers who are fully alive in the Holy Spirit. It is our portion to move in the Holy Spirit so we are going to have the fierce, warrior-like courage of the lion; we are going to have the reliable, servant spirit of the ox; the dignity of the man who has the privilege of fellowshipping with the Trinity; and the anointing to fly high like the eagle into supernatural realms of glory. The Holy Spirit will release all of these dimensions in the midst of the people of God in the kingdom.

These living creatures are closest to the throne of God, and they see a glimpse of God's beauty. It is so overwhelming that with two of their six wings, they cover their eyes, and they bow down and cry day and night, "Holy, holy, holy," which is the same thing as saying, "Transcendent beauty, transcendent beauty, transcendent beauty."

The living creatures have been around the throne much longer than mankind, and they never tire of being in God's presence. It is like they are a prophetic statement that God's beauty is inexhaustible. We will never tire of seeing Him or of being in His presence.

WHAT CAN I DO?

Begin your prayer time by picturing yourself in the throne scene. The fire of the Spirit is hovering over you. You're looking at the Father as He emanates with the diamond-like brilliance of jasper and the red sardius that points to His fiery love. The emerald rainbow over Him declares His mercy. There are a myriad of angels in the atmosphere and the four living creatures around the Father's face saying, "Holy, holy, holy." The twenty-four elders are falling before Him in lovesick adoration. And you are there too, crying, "Holy, holy, holy," with the saints on the sea of glass because He is worthy.

FOR REFLECTION

"Whenever the living creatures give glory and honor and thanks to Him who sits on the throne, who lives forever and ever, the twenty-four elders fall down before Him who sits on the throne and worship Him who lives forever and ever, and cast their crowns before the throne, saying: "You are worthy, O Lord, to receive glory and honor and power; for You created all things, and by Your will they exist and were created" (Rev. 4:9–11).

> *Lord, my heart burns for You. As glorious and humbling as the scene around Your throne is, I will not draw back from Your presence. I will draw near to You and proclaim Your love in the earth.*

Day 97

Contending for a Third Great Awakening

*Every great movement of God can
be traced to a kneeling figure.*

—D. L. MOODY

I BELIEVE ONE PLAN God has is to send another great awakening to America and the nations of the earth, and I am contending in prayer for just such a great move of God. In both the First and Second Great Awakenings in America in the eighteenth and nineteenth centuries, massive numbers of people came to the Lord as the result of an unusual measure of the power of conviction on the preaching of the Word. We have seen the role the spirit of prayer played in releasing this power.

But during the twentieth century, there was no such awakening in America. Yes, there was the move of the Holy Spirit at Azusa Street that led to the Pentecostal and Charismatic movements, but there was no widespread release of the conviction of the Holy Spirit on the preaching of the Word and no large numbers of new converts who walked in purity and the fear of the Lord for years.

I am thankful to God for the Jesus Movement in the 1970s, when many young people were born again. I was saved during that time. But again, in this movement we did not see the spirit of conviction with the fear of the Lord being released across entire cities and regions.

It has been almost 150 years since our nation has seen a great awakening. However, a great awakening is coming to America again, one that will far surpass the previous two and go beyond all that happened at Azusa Street, in the Jesus Movement, and as a result of the Pentecostal, Charismatic, and various regional renewal movements. I am desperate for true revival, and I will never be satisfied with anything less than a full measure of what God is willing to give. If you have the same vision and desire, continue to petition Him in faith and hope, enter in to the spirit of prayer when it comes upon you, and then give yourself fully to it. It is good to pray for your own local church or college ministry, but I encourage you to focus your prayer on something bigger—that is, revival for your *entire region* or for a Third Great Awakening across our nation. I assure you that, in the process of answering your "big" prayer, God will not forget to touch us.

WHAT CAN I DO?

Get involved in ministry at your church so that you grow in ministry experience and cultivate faithfulness that prepares you for the great outpouring God is bringing upon the whole earth.

FOR REFLECTION

"Repent, therefore, and reform your lives, so that the record of your sins may be cancelled, and that there may come seasons of revival from the Lord" (Acts 3:19, WEY).

> *Lord, I stand in agreement with my brothers and sisters in Christ as we contend for a great outpouring of Your Spirit—a Third Great Awakening. Revive us again, Lord!*

_____

_____

_____

_____

_____

Prayer and Worship Are Intertwined in God's Plan

There has never been a spiritual awakening in any country or locality that did not begin in united prayer.

—A. T. Pierson

THE HOLY SPIRIT wants to establish a culture of prayer integrated with worship in the church. In fact, He is currently raising up the greatest prayer and worship movement in history. Why? Because engaging in worship and intercession is the primary means by which He releases His power on the earth in this age and in the age to come. Worship and intercession are among the few things that we do both now and forever.

Prayer and worship have always been at the center of God's purpose. We see how central this is in God's government—He established 24/7 worship and prayer in His royal court where He reigns on His sovereign throne (Rev. 4:8). Human history actually began in a "prayer meeting" in the Garden of Eden as Adam walked with God each day in the cool of the day (Gen. 3:8).

Israel, as a nation, also began at a fiery "prayer meeting" at Mount Sinai, which was ablaze with God's fire, after the people crossed the Red Sea. At that time God called them to be a kingdom of priests (Exod. 19:6–20). The first assignment He gave Israel as a nation under Moses' leadership was to build a worship sanctuary, a house of prayer, in the wilderness (Exod. 25). Jesus Himself began His public ministry in a prayer meeting in the wilderness (Matt. 4) and ended it in a prayer meeting in the Garden of Gethsemane (Matt. 26). The early church began in a prayer meeting in the Upper Room as Jesus' followers waited for "the Promise of the Father" (Acts 1:4).

Natural history, as we know it, will end in the context of a global prayer movement. The conflict at the end of the age will be between two houses of prayer, two global worship movements—one worshipping Jesus and the other worshipping the Antichrist.

Today the Holy Spirit is raising up what will become the most powerful worship movement in history.[1] It will totally defeat the Antichrist's end-time worship movement. (See Revelation 13 and 19:19–21.) The Scripture makes it clear that worship and intercession are of great value to the Lord in heaven, on earth in this age, and on earth in the age to come.

WHAT CAN I DO?

If your church doesn't already schedule regular prayer meetings, ask the leadership if such a meeting could be planned in the next month. It's OK to start small; just start.

FOR REFLECTION

"Yes, all kings shall fall down before Him; all nations shall serve Him" (Ps. 72:11).

Lord, make my life a continual prayer meeting before You, and bring those of like spirit across my path so we can join together to see "thy kingdom come" on earth.

_____

_____

_____

_____

_____

Day 99

The Anna Calling: Intercessory Missionary

What the church needs today is not more machinery or better, not new organizations or more and novel methods, but men whom the Holy Spirit can use—men of prayer, men mighty in prayer.

—E. M. Bounds

SOME PEOPLE ASK me where intercessory missionaries are found in the New Testament. My response: Where in the New Testament do we find leaders who do *not* prioritize prayer? Beginning with Jesus and the apostles, the New Testament highlights many leaders who gave themselves to prayer in an extravagant way.

One of the most powerful examples in the New Testament of an intercessory missionary is Anna, an elderly Jewish widow who prayed in the temple night and day prior to Jesus' birth. She was empowered by the grace of God to spend long hours in His presence for many years (see Luke 2:36–38).

Anna was a "watchman" set on the wall in Jerusalem. We see in her an expression of Isaiah's prophecy: "All day and all night" she "never kept silent" (Isa. 62:6, NASB). Through Isaiah, the Lord promised to set intercessors in place for His end-time purposes, and Anna was a token of what will happen across the nations during the generation in which the Lord returns.

Anna is representative of intercessors with grace to sustain long hours of prayer for many years. Her calling—what I refer to as "the Anna calling"—transcends gender and age. *It is for male and female, young and old.* When I refer to an intercessory missionary as having a specific "Anna calling," I mean he or she has grace for much prayer and fasting.

In this very hour the Lord is wooing those with a heart and a calling like Anna's to the full-time occupation of worship and prayer. He is personally appointing them and setting them in their places. The Lord is calling forth modern-day people like Anna in churches and prayer rooms around the world, and we must celebrate them as a great gift to the body of Christ and the prayer movement, recognizing and releasing them to obey their God-given mandates.

The greatest ministry is to do the will of God, whatever that may be for each one of us. In other words, the greatest ministry you can have is the one to which God calls *you.* The pressure of trying to operate in another's calling leads to all types of problems, including burnout, disappointment, and discouragement. So I urge you: do not despise your calling, and do not try to imitate the ministry of another. Embrace your own individual calling, whether it is serving God full time in the marketplace; in your home, school, or neighborhood; or in the prayer movement, because it is the highest calling for you.

WHAT CAN I DO?

Ask God to bring those with an Anna calling across your path, and band together for intercession. Even if your gathering (physical or by phone) numbers only two or three people, you will accomplish much for the kingdom.

FOR REFLECTION

"We will give ourselves continually to prayer and to the ministry of the word" (Acts 6:4).

Lord, I set my heart to be a watchman on the wall, an intercessor who is available for Your leading, attuned to Your prompting, and willing to obey Your call.

Day 100

The Vow That Changed History

All great revivals have been preceded and carried out by persevering, prevailing knee-work in the closet.

—Samuel Brengle

PSALM 132 RECORDS a vow of King David that is at the heart of the end-time missions and prayer movement. I call it *"the vow that changed history"* because dedicated believers throughout the ages have embraced the spirit of it and set their hearts to live by it. The vow is a commitment to be wholehearted in seeking the fullness of God's purpose and release of His presence.

> "Surely I will not go into the chamber of my house, or go up to the comfort of my bed; I will not give sleep to my eyes or slumber to my eyelids, until I find a place for the LORD, a dwelling place for the Mighty One of Jacob."...Arise, O, LORD, to Your resting place.
>
> —Psalm 132:2–5, 8

David's heart was gripped with something bigger than his personal comfort and promotion. As a young man he vowed to dedicate his life to finding a "resting place" or "dwelling place" for God. Both phrases speak of the same reality. In principle a "dwelling place" speaks of a place (a city or region) where God's purpose is done to the fullest measure ordained by God in any given generation and where His presence is manifested on earth in a way that is discernable even to unbelievers.

David's vow included establishing day-and-night worship by setting singers and musicians in place to join him in contending for the fullness of God's purpose in their generation. The apostle Paul described David as a man who served the fullness of God's purpose, doing all His will in his generation (Acts 13:22, 36).

In a spiritual sense the church on earth is the dwelling place of God today, and we can contend for a much greater release of God's presence now through the worldwide body of Christ. Thus a "dwelling place for the Lord" may in principle describe a community of believers who walk in the fear of the Lord with the first commandment in first place in their lives and who obey with gratitude and humility. They will see demonstrations of God's power with signs and wonders so that many come to know the Lord in a deep and glorious way.

Remaining faithful to his vow brought reproach on David. He was mocked because he boldly stood for what God was zealous for in his generation. His family and friends told jokes about him because of the intensity with which he sought God. The spiritual and political leaders in his community—those who sat at the gate of the city—spoke against him. Even the drunkards mocked him with songs that criticized his zeal for God.

Some sincere believers draw back from zealously seeking God due to fear of receiving criticism from others. They cannot bear the reproach that comes as a result of diligently pursuing Him. Some draw back because of the love of comfort—they want things to be easier. Some draw back because they want more money—seeking God takes time away from earning an income.

Does David's vow and vision for a dwelling place stir your heart? Many dedicated believers throughout church history have embraced the spirit of David's vow. All through the ages the Lord has raised up groups that function as a radical core of holy, praying believers. These groups may be as small as five to ten or as large as several hundred. There are undoubtedly many groups like this in your city in various churches with different denominational affiliations. Surely you want to be a part of one!

Find out what God is doing in your generation and then fully throw yourself into it. Determine to be a part of a radical core that will not stop until the fullness of God's purpose is released. Be a revivalist or part of a "revival company" that is fully dedicated to Jesus.

WHAT CAN I DO?

Become a dwelling place for the Lord. Declare your intention to the Father, and rejoice as He sets up His resting place in your life.

FOR REFLECTION

"In whom you also are being built together for a dwelling place of God in the Spirit" (Eph. 2:22).

> *Lord, make my heart a dwelling place for Your Spirit, and cause my church to be Your resting place so that You can accomplish Your will for our community.*

_____

_____

_____

_____

_____

_____

_____

_____

_____

_____

Notes

DAY 11

1.   As quoted in Thomas Dubay, *Faith and Certitude* (San Francisco: Ignatius Press, 1985). Dubay is quoting a statement made by a character in Fyodor Dostoyevsky's novel *The Brothers Karamazov.*

DAY 12

1.   As quoted in Thomas Dubay, *The Evidential Power of Beauty: Science and Theology Meet* (San Francisco: Ignatius Press, 1999), 14. Dubay is quoting from Book I of *St. Augustine's Confessions.*

DAY 38

1.   Basil Miller, *George Müller: Man of Faith and Miracles* (Minneapolis, MN: Bethany House Publishers, 1941), 146.

DAY 43

1.   Goodreads.com, "John Calvin Quotes," accessed July 18, 2018, https://www.goodreads.com/author/quotes/30510.John_Calvin.

DAY 98

1.   See Isaiah 62:6–7; 24:14–16; 25:9; 26:8–9; 30:18–19; 42:10–13; Luke 18:7–8; Revelation 22:17; 5:8; 8:4.

MIKE BICKLE
TEACHING LIBRARY

—— *Free Teaching & Resource Library* ——

This International House of Prayer resource library, encompassing more than 25 years of Mike's teaching ministry, provides access to hundreds of resources in various formats, including streaming video, downloadable video, and audio, accompanied by study notes and transcriptions, absolutely free of charge.

You will find some of Mike's most requested titles, including *The Life of David, The First Commandment, Jesus, Our Magnificent Obsession, The Book of Romans, The Book of Revelation,* and much more.

We encourage you to freely copy any of these teachings to share with others or use in any way: "our copyright is the right to copy." Older messages are continually being prepared and uploaded from Mike's archives, and all new teachings will be added immediately.

Visit mikebickle.org

International House of Prayer Missions Base, 3535 E. Red Bridge Road, Kansas City, MO 64137
(816) 763-0200 | info@ihopkc.org | ihopkc.org

International House *of* Prayer

INTERNSHIPS

ENCOUNTER GOD. DO HIS WORKS. CHANGE THE WORLD.
ihopkc.org/internships

Each of our five internships are committed to praying for the release of the fullness of God's power and purpose, as interns actively win the lost, heal the sick, feed the poor, and minister in the power of the Holy Spirit. Our vision is to work in relationship with the larger Body of Christ to serve the Great Commission, as we seek to walk out the two great commandments to love God and people. Our desire is to see each intern build strong relationships and lifelong friendships.

INTRO TO IHOPKC
Two three-month tracks designed to impart the vision and values of the International House of Prayer, along with the practical skills necessary to succeed long-term as an intercessory missionary. For singles, couples, and families. Classes for children available.

FIRE IN THE NIGHT
Come and behold the beauty of Jesus in the night hours. Grow in love for God and take your stand in intercession as a watchman of the night. Fire in the Night is for young adults, ages 18–30.

ONE THING INTERNSHIP
A six-month residential program for single young adults, ages 18 to 25.

SIMEON COMPANY
Two three-month tracks for over-50s, married or single.

HOPE CITY INTERNSHIP
A three-month internship program equipping intercessory missionaries to minister in the inner city, serve in the soup kitchen, lead in our inner-city prayer room, and minister to gang members, drug addicts, and the homeless.

International House of Prayer Missions Base, 3535 E. Red Bridge Road, Kansas City, MO 64137
(816) 763-0200 | info@ihopkc.org | ihopkc.org